"Christopher Emdin's *For White Folks Who Teach in the Hood . . . and the Rest of Y'all Too* is a brilliant, blistering, and bracing call to arms for those who teach and learn in urban America. Pivoting effortlessly from street vernacular to sophisticated theory without losing the common touch—or the lovely language and lucid thought—Emdin reminds us that the children and young people who throng our urban schools are worthy of every attempt to sharpen their minds and prepare them for a satisfying life far beyond the classroom. If you're looking for the revolutionary meaning, and imaginative transformation, of teaching for the *real* America, you're holding it in your hands! Christopher Emdin is Jonathan Kozol with swag!"

—Michael Eric Dyson, author of *The Black Presidency: Barack Obama and the Politics of Race in America*

"Christopher Emdin's *For White Folks Who Teach in the Hood . . . and the Rest of Y'all Too* is essential reading for all adults who work with black and brown young people. In crisp and elegant form, he brilliantly weaves together an archive of literary, academic, and what he terms 'neoindigenous' forms of knowledge to develop critical theory. Emdin draws upon the intellectual and creative gifts that emerge from the students and their traditions and challenges, and unravels the widespread fiction that they are incapable, unprepared, and uninterested in school. Ultimately, he sets forth best pedagogical practices to replace ones that repeatedly fail. Throughout, Emdin shares his own revelatory personal narrative as a student and educator in vivid and captivating detail. His prose is engaging, poignant, and humorous at times, and his book is accessible and broadly appealing. Yet it is also filled with exceptional intellectual sophistication and necessary wisdom for the future of education."

—Imani Perry, author of *Prophets of the Hood: Politics and Poetics in Hip Hop*

"For White Folks Who Teach in the Hood . . . and the Rest of Y'all Too is an important addition to the field of teacher education. From hip-hop to high theory, the journey Christopher Emdin takes us on is at once critical and compassionate, analytical and actionable. Through rich stories and well-developed frameworks, *For White Folks* offers a compelling and accessible road map for anyone (not just white folks!) teaching twenty-first century urban youth. It also confirms Christopher Emdin's reputation as one of the most important education scholars of our generation."

—Marc Lamont Hill, author of *Beats, Rhymes, and Classroom Life: Hip-Hop Pedagogy and the Politics of Identity* and Distinguished Professor of Africana Studies at Morehouse College

"A generation ago Ntzoke Shange gave us a 'choreopoem.' Today, Christopher Emdin offers us a 'pedagopoem.' This volume is a powerful dance of teaching and art. It engages both the art and science of what teachers must do to be successful with all students. It is simultaneously lyrical and analytic, scientific and humanistic, a work of the heart and the mind. It belongs in every teacher's library!"

—Gloria Ladson-Billings, the Kellner Family Distinguished Chair in Urban Education, University of Wisconsin–Madison

For White Folks Who Teach in the Hood
. . . and the Rest of Y'all Too

For White Folks Who Teach in the Hood

. . . and the Rest of Y'all Too

Reality Pedagogy and Urban Education

Christopher Emdin

A Simmons College/Beacon Press
Race, Education, and Democracy Series Book

BEACON PRESS
BOSTON

BEACON PRESS
Boston, Massachusetts
www.beacon.org

Beacon Press books
are published under the auspices of
the Unitarian Universalist Association of Congregations.

This book is published as part of the Simmons College/Beacon Press Race, Education, and Democracy Lecture and Book Series and is based on lectures delivered at Simmons College in 2014.

20 19 18   14 13 12 11 10   (cloth)
20 19 18   12 11 10 9   (pbk.)

This book is printed on acid-free paper that meets the uncoated paper ANSI/NISO specifications for permanence as revised in 1992.

Text design and composition by Kim Arney

Library of Congress Cataloging-in-Publication Data

Names: Emdin, Christopher, author.
Title: For white folks who teach in the hood . . . and the rest of y'all too :
  reality pedagogy and urban education / Christopher Emdin.
Description: Boston, Massachusetts : Beacon Press, 2016.
Identifiers: LCCN 2015033466 | ISBN 978-0-8070-0640-5 (hardcover) |
  ISBN 978-0-8070-2802-5 (paperback) | ISBN 978-0-8070-0641-2 (ebook)
Subjects: LCSH: Education, Urban—United States—Sociological aspects. |
  Hip-hop—United States—Influence. | BISAC: EDUCATION / Teaching
  Methods & Materials / Science & Technology. | EDUCATION / Philosophy &
  Social Aspects. | EDUCATION / Multicultural Education.
Classification: LCC LC5131 .E5 2016 | DDC 370.9173/2—dc23 LC record
available at http://lccn.loc.gov/2015033466

Contents

Preface

I have always been fascinated by the brilliant theater piece *For Colored Girls Who Have Considered Suicide / When the Rainbow Is Enuf*, by Ntozake Shange. I was first drawn to this powerful work by its colorful cover, and I fell in love with it when I began to read the powerful prose. As a teenager, it was the title that affected me most. Seeing the word *enuf* in print, on the cover of a book, meant the world to me. It was bold and provocative—and it comforted me to know that someone from outside the four-block radius I called home knew this word. *Enuf* and *enough* are very different words. They have the same meaning, can be used in the same context, but each has very different significance to those who employ them. *Enuf* sits comfortably in the subtitle of a book like *For Colored Girls Who Have Considered Suicide*, allowing the work to call out to those for and about whom it is written. Its presence in the book title indicates that there is no political correctness, no tainting of the truth, and no hiding of what needs to be said. It prepares the reader for the substance of the text.

In many ways, this book draws from the traditions set forth by Shange. While it is neither a collection of poems and stories nor a theater piece, its intentions are similar. The title works toward invoking necessary truths and offering new ways forward. It is clearly intended for "white folks who teach in the hood." But it is also for those who work with them, hire them, whose family members are taught by them, and who themselves are being, or have been, taught by them.

In short, this book is for people of all colors who take a particular approach to education. They may be white. They may be black. In all cases, they are so deeply committed to an approach to pedagogy that is Eurocentric in its form and function that the color of their skin doesn't matter. When I say that their skin color doesn't matter, I am not dismissing the particular responsibilities of privileged groups in societies that disadvantage marginalized groups. I am also not discounting the need to discuss race and injustice under the fallacy of equity. What I am suggesting is that it is possible for people of all racial and ethnic backgrounds to take on approaches to teaching that hurt youth of color. Malcolm X described this phenomenon in a powerful speech about the house Negro and the field Negro in the slave South. He described the black slave who toiled in the fields and the house Negro who worked in the white master's house. He noted that at some point, the house Negro became so invested in the well-being of the master that the master's needs and concerns took preeminence over his own needs and that of the field Negro. This is the equivalent of the black educator so invested in the structure and pedagogies of the traditional school system that the needs of black and brown students become secondary to maintaining the status quo. For the "white" educator, this investment in traditional schooling is often generational, following the beliefs of parents and grandparents with college degrees and ideas about what school should look like. The point here is that there are both black and white people who can be classified as "white folks"—in that they maintain a system that doesn't serve the needs of youth in the hood.

"The hood" is often identified as a place where dysfunction is prevalent and people need to be saved from themselves and their circumstances. The hood may be urban, rural, densely or sparsely populated, but it has a number of shared characteristics that make it easy to recognize. The community is often socioeconomically disadvantaged, achievement gaps are prevalent, and a very particular brand of pedagogy is normalized. In these communities, and particularly in urban schools, African American and Latino youth are most hard hit by poverty and its aftereffects. For example, in Atlanta, 80 percent of African American children have been reported to live in conditions of high poverty, compared with 29 percent of their Asian peers and 6 percent of their white peers. In fact, the largest twenty school districts in the nation enroll 80 percent minority students, compared with 42 percent in all school districts. In cities like Los Angeles, Chicago, and Miami, urban schools enroll less than 10 percent Anglo students, even though the teachers are overwhelmingly white. In New York public schools, over 70 percent of high school youth are students of color, while over 80 percent of public high school teachers in the state are white.

While some may use these statistics to push for more minority teachers, I argue that there must also be a concerted effort to improve the teaching of white teachers who are already teaching in these schools, as well as those who aspire to teach there, to challenge the "white folks' pedagogy" that is being practiced by teachers of all ethnic and racial backgrounds.

Commencement

I sank, exhausted, into the backseat of a small sport utility vehicle as it pulled onto a sparsely populated Wyoming highway, finally getting some rest after a long day. As I opened the window to get some air, the desert breeze awakened me to the most beautiful sunset I had ever witnessed. The sky was a mix of purple, blue, and pale orange, made even more vivid by the light brown dust on the side of the road and the gray asphalt stretching out ahead. Soaking up that beautiful sky, I thought about the teachers I had met that day. They were mostly white middle and high school teachers who taught science and mathematics to Native American students. I had been invited to Wyoming to deliver a lecture about ways to improve teaching and learning in science, technology, engineering, and mathematics (STEM), and spent almost forty-five minutes after the hourlong lecture answering a host of questions about strategies for engaging students and teaching them more effectively.

As I marveled at the passing scenery, two things occurred to me. The first was that these teachers had a genuine love and concern for their students. If they didn't, they wouldn't have shown up at my lecture and asked so many questions. The second thought, which seemed initially to be unrelated to the first, was that I was driving over land that belonged to the same Indigenous Americans whose descendants

I was preparing these white educators to teach. As the colors of the sky slowly deepened, I thought again about the follow-up questions the teachers had asked: How do we get disinterested students to care about themselves and their education? Why are our students not excited about learning? Why aren't they adjusting well to the rules of school? Why are they underperforming academically? These questions were remarkably similar to the ones the mostly white teachers in my workshops in urban areas like New York City, Chicago, and Los Angeles routinely asked me. Apparently, they mattered here in Wyoming as well.

I had done my best to address the teachers' questions carefully and consider their evident frustrations. In an effort to not offend, I steered clear of the elephant in the room—that is, the very obvious racial and ethnic differences between these mostly white teachers and their mostly Indigenous American students. Instead I shared a number of teaching strategies that I knew from experience worked for all students. I mentioned hands-on activities and guided inquiry in science, real-life applications and modeling in mathematics, and ways to incorporate writing across the curriculum. As I shared these strategies, I felt like I was connecting with the teachers. I had given them new information and helped them to approach their classes differently. After the lecture, many thanked me for my words and suggestions. A few even asked for links to articles so that they could learn more. That's usually a good sign. I was content that the lecture had gone well, and I reveled in that feeling as I left to embark on the next phase of my trip.

But now, traveling through the Wyoming landscape, it struck me that although the teachers had gained insight about their profession, it wouldn't be much help to them if they didn't fully understand their students. I had given them tools to pacify their concerns, but nothing to truly get to the root of their problems. After all was said and done, I wasn't sure that the teachers knew or cared about the origin of their challenges: the vast divide that existed between the traditional schools in which they taught and the unique culture of their students.

That afternoon, I was reminded of the book *My People the Sioux* by Indigenous American writer Luther Standing Bear. In this book, which was published in 1928, Standing Bear describes the beauty of the Sioux territory, the very land I was now traveling through. Long before I visited Wyoming, sitting on a park bench in the Bronx, Standing Bear's words had both physically and intellectually transported me to this place. When I read his book, I saw in my mind the physical landscape that now surrounded me. The skies, the sun, and the clouds felt familiar. More importantly, his illuminating words enabled me to draw connections between the teaching and learning of populations like Indigenous Americans and the urban youth of color in my hometown.

Lessons from the Sioux

With the rumbling of a New York City commuter train above, and the Bronx skyline before me, I read Standing Bear and became fascinated with the ways of the Sioux. His stories of Native American life and the unique traditions of his people reminded me of my youth in East Flatbush, Brooklyn, and in the Bronx. As he described the distinct codes and rules of engagement of his people, I saw analogous images from the hip-hop generation. In one memorable passage he describes a solemn occasion commemorating a death, where a Sioux elder holds the bowl of a smoking pipe first to the heavens, then to the east, south, west, and north, and finally down, in the direction of Mother Earth. Reading this, all I could think of was the men in my urban neighborhood who lift liquor in brown paper bags to the heavens and to the earth in times of sorrow or to memorialize a member of the community. As a young man, I had always been fascinated by this lifting up and pouring of liquor "for the brothers who ain't here" by older members of the community. At the time, I couldn't identify why I was drawn to this practice, but I knew it signified something powerful. The meaning didn't become clear until I read Standing Bear's words about the role of elders, reverence for the land, and the powerful community practices around sorrow and healing. His descriptions of the Sioux opened up and deepened my understandings of life in the Bronx.

In his book, Luther Standing Bear poignantly describes his experience as a student at the Carlisle Indian Industrial School—the first institution designed to "educate the Indian." Established in 1879 in Carlisle, Pennsylvania, the school was founded by Richard Henry Pratt, a US Army officer who had served in the Indian Wars and believed that his experience with the Native peoples he had formerly captured and imprisoned equipped him to educate them. The white teachers he recruited sincerely believed in Pratt's vision. For them, it was because of Pratt's genuine concern for the Indigenous Americans that he had found it in his heart to give them a better life through education. It was this idealism that led educators to leave positions at other schools to be a part of the experiment to "tame the Wild Indian."

The Carlisle School employed a militaristic approach to "helping" the Indigenous Americans assimilate to white norms. For students, the authoritarian "care" that was shown to them at school stripped them of their culture and traditions, considered primitive and inferior. Unfortunately, because many of these students were far from the support of their Native communities, they were forced to assimilate to the culture of the teachers and the school so as to avoid the harsh punishments that would otherwise be levied on them. As the teachers worked to "tame and train" students who were described as "savage beasts," students struggled to maintain their authenticity amid the efforts to make them "as close to the White man as possible."[1] This tension between educators who saw themselves as kindhearted people who were doing right by the less fortunate, and students who struggled to maintain their culture and identity while being forced to be the type of student their teachers envisioned, played a part in the eventual recognition that the Carlisle School was a failed experiment.

The teachers who were recruited to the Carlisle School were in many ways like white folks who teach in the hood today. Written accounts from that era confirm that Carlisle teachers saw themselves as caring professionals, even though students described many of them as overly strict and mean-spirited disciplinarians. One teacher wrote in the school paper, *The Red Man*, that the students had "unevenly developed characters, strong idiosyncrasies and a lack of systematic home training." His only praise for the indigenous students was their "native unconscious keenness." Another teacher described a teaching culture in which "the students are under constant discipline from which there is no appeal."[2] This culture of unrelenting discipline was presented by educators as benefiting the Carlisle School's challenging population. The Carlisle system had a goal to "make students better," but this goal was predicated on the teachers' understanding that the students came to the school lacking in socialization, intellect, and worth. The school celebrated teachers' rigidity and strictness out of a belief that this was the type of training that would be successful in acculturating indigenous students to white society.

The use of strong discipline with respect to "challenging" youth continues to be celebrated today, as illustrated by a highly publicized video in April 2015, during the protests that erupted in Baltimore, Maryland, in response to the death of a young black man while in police custody. In the video, the child's mother is recorded beating and cursing at her son for taking part in the protest. While it is obvious from the recording that the mother was concerned for her child and maybe even feared for his safety, she showed this concern by berating him in public. The media praised the "riot mom" for how she addressed the situation—she was widely hailed as "Mother of the Year"—but in so doing perpetuated the narrative of young black boys requiring a tough hand to keep them in line.

Consider a teacher who graduates from a teacher-preparation program and has job prospects at both an affluent suburban school and what can be described as a poor urban school. Before the teacher can consider the two jobs, she must reckon with certain criteria beyond content knowledge, academic credentials, and teaching experience. In the more affluent schools, one's ability to teach the subject material is prioritized, and so is a caring temperament. In this case, care is demonstrated by a teacher's patience and dedication to teaching.

In urban communities that are populated by youth of color, there are other, and oftentimes unwritten, expectations like having strong classroom-management skills and not being a pushover. In this case, care is expressed through "tough love."

In my role as a teacher-educator, I often give an assignment to aspiring teachers that includes writing an autobiography and teaching statement to explore what brought them to the field of education. For those who go on to work in urban schools, I am always fascinated by the ways that these teachers' descriptions of themselves and their craft highlight their concern for urban youth, empathy for their living conditions, and a desire to help them have more opportunities. As I watch them transition from aspiring teachers to practitioners, I see how this "care for the other" couples with expectations of managing and disciplining students, and the ways that they unintentionally become modern incarnations of the instructors at the Carlisle School through a tough-love approach to pedagogy. As I follow these teachers into classrooms and study the ways they interact with their students, I find that the students' descriptions of their schools and teachers are similar to the ways that Indigenous Americans at Carlisle described their schooling experiences. Many urban youth of color describe oppressive places that have a primary goal of imposing rules and maintaining control. Urban youth in contemporary America use language similar to Carlisle students like Standing Bear and student turned teacher Zitkala-Sa, who highlighted the ways that the school disrespected the students and their home cultures. These students' words stand in sharp contrast to those of their teachers as expressed in autobiographies and teaching philosophies.

The ideology of the Carlisle School is alive and well in contemporary urban school policies. These include zero tolerance and lockdown procedures. A student in a school I recently visited described the innocuous term *school safety* as a "nice-sounding code word for treating you like you're in jail or something." In urban school districts across the country, school safety personnel are uniformed officers who are part of the police force and often engage in discriminatory practices that reflect those in the larger community.

Like teachers who were drawn to the Carlisle School, white teachers are recruited to work in poor communities of color through programs like Teach for America, which tout their exclusivity and draw teachers from privileged cultural and educational backgrounds to teach in the hood. These programs attract teachers to urban and rural schools by emphasizing the poor resources and low socioeconomic status of these schools rather than the assets of the community. Adages like "No child should be left back from a quality education" and "Be something bigger than yourself" draw well-intentioned teachers desiring to save poor kids from their despairing circumstances. This is not a critique of Teach for America per se—as it serves a need in urban and rural communities. However, it and programs like it tend to exoticize the schools they serve and downplay the assets and strengths of the communities they are seeking to improve. I argue that if aspiring teachers from these programs were challenged to teach with an acknowledgment of, and respect for, the local knowledge of urban communities, and were made aware of how the models for teaching and recruitment they are a part of reinforce a tradition that does not do right by students, they could be strong assets for urban communities. However, because of their unwillingness to challenge the traditions and structures from which they were borne, efforts that recruit teachers for urban schools ensure that Carlisle-type practices continue to exist.

A fundamental step in this challenging of structures is to think about new ways for all education stakeholders—particularly those who are not from the communities in which they teach—to engage with urban youth of color. What new lenses or frameworks can we use to bring white folks who teach in the hood to consider that urban education is more complex than saving students and being a hero? I suggest a way forward by making deep connections between the indigenous and urban youth of color.

Connecting the Indigenous and Neoindigenous

The United Nations Declaration on the Rights of Indigenous Peoples defines the indigenous as people whose existence in a certain geographic location predates the region's conquering or occupation by a colonial or imperialist power, and who see themselves as, or have been positioned as, separate from those who are politically or socially in command of the region. This definition, while it glosses over the nuances of what it means to be indigenous, nevertheless provides an outline and lays out the criteria for understanding who is and who isn't indigenous. It touches upon indigenous peoples' close ties to their land, their physical and mental colonization, and their position as distinct from those who govern them. It posits that the indigenous have their own unique ways of constructing knowledge, utilize distinct modes of communication in their interactions with one another, and hold cultural understandings that vary from the established norm. Above all, the UN definition of the indigenous speaks to the collective oppression that a population experiences at the hands of a more powerful and dominant group.

When we think of the Indigenous American students of the Carlisle School, the UN definition fits perfectly. However, when this definition is stripped of its explicit association with geographic locations, it's clear that it can be applied to marginalized populations generally. Because of the similarities in experience between the indigenous and urban youth of color, I identify urban youth as *neoindigenous*. This connection between the indigenous and neoindigenous follows from what Benedict Anderson, professor of International Studies at Cornell University, describes as imagined communities that transcend place and time, and connect groups of people based on their shared experiences.[3]

I first articulated the need for positioning urban youth as neoindigenous in a paper written for the American Association for the Advancement of Curriculum Studies in 2005. Since then, I've heard the term used loosely by academics in reference to the direct ancestors of those traditionally referred to as indigenous[4] and also to a very specific Asian worldview.[5] While multiple interpretations of what it means to be neoindigenous have value for understanding contemporary forms of oppression and expression, identifying contemporary indigenous as neoindigenous merely effects a renaming. For example,

Aboriginal Australians have inhabited that continent for some fifty thousand years. Recasting contemporary Aboriginal Australians as neoindigenous extracts them from their history and attempts to restart it. On the other hand, positioning urban marginalized youth as neoindigenous moves beyond a literal biological or geographical connection and into more complex connections among the oppressed that call forth a particular way of looking at the world. Identifying urban youth of color as neoindigenous allows us to understand the oppression these youth experience, the spaces they inhabit, and the ways these phenomena affect what happens in social settings like traditional classrooms. It seeks to position these youth in a larger context of marginalization, displacement, and diaspora.

Like the indigenous, the neoindigenous are a group that will not fade into oblivion despite attempts to rename or relocate them. The term *neoindigenous* carries the rich histories of indigenous groups, acknowledges powerful connections among populations that have dealt with being silenced, and signals the need to examine the ways that institutions replicate colonial processes. The neoindigenous will continue to exist, and need to be acknowledged, in classrooms for as long as traditional teaching promotes an imaginary white middle-class ideal. As long as white middle-class teachers are recruited to schools occupied by urban youth of color, without any consideration of how they affirm and reestablish power dynamics that silence students, issues that plague urban education (like achievement gaps, suspension rates, and high teacher turnover) will persist.

The neoindigenous often look, act, and engage in the classroom in ways that are inconsistent with traditional school norms. Like the indigenous, they are viewed as intellectually and academically deficient to their counterparts from other racial and socioeconomic backgrounds. Too often, when these students speak or interact in the classroom in ways that teachers are uncomfortable with, they are categorized as troubled students, or diagnosed with disorders like ADD (attention deficit disorder) and ODD (oppositional defiant disorder). The Association for Psychological Science recently shared a study finding that black students were more likely to be labeled as troublemakers by their teachers and treated harshly in classrooms.[6] Students who are treated harshly in classrooms are less likely to academically engage in classrooms, which results in their being perceived as academically inferior. For teachers to acknowledge that the ways they perceive, group, and diagnose students has a dramatic impact on student outcomes, moves them toward reconciling the cultural differences they have with students, a significant step toward changing the way educators engage with urban youth of color.

Addressing the cultural differences between teachers and students requires what educational researcher Gloria Ladson-Billings describes as culturally relevant pedagogy.[7] This approach to teaching advocates for a consideration of the culture of the students in determining the ways in which they are taught. Unfortunately, this approach cannot be implemented unless teachers broaden their scope beyond traditional classroom teaching.

Cultural artifacts like clothing, music, or speech are aspects of indigenous culture that are generally not considered by teachers to be related to education, but are one of the first things a teacher identifies when interacting with neoindigenous students. The wrong clothing or speech will get neoindigenous students labeled as unwilling to learn and directly impact their academic lives much in the way that it affects the indigenous. For example, if one were to ask the average person in the United States, Australia, or New Zealand to describe the indigenous peoples in their respective countries, the responses would probably be very similar, and include exoticized references to scanty clothing, "odd" living arrangements, "strange" speech, "weird" customs, and "primitive" art and music.

Educational anthropologist Rosemary Henze, in her work with Kathryn Davis, describes the indigenous languages of Australia and New Zealand as having much complexity and nuance despite the fact that they are generally perceived as substandard in the countries where they are spoken.[8] In much the same way, educators perceive neoindigenous Spanglish (a mixing of Spanish and English) or patois as substandard. On a number of occasions, I've heard teachers mock neoindigenous slang in front of students, even while they themselves attempt to use it in an effort to look cool or gain "street cred" in other settings. A white female urban schoolteacher from an affluent background once told me that whenever she gets together with her friends, they say she's "been in the ghetto with the black kids for too long" because of her frequent use of "street slang." She giggled as she admitted that she sometimes "uses the kids' phrases on purpose" to get a reaction from her friends. This teacher, like many of her peers, exoticizes neoindigenous language, but still holds a general perception that it represents lowbrow antiacademic culture. Ironically, when teachers try to use neoindigenous language, they often find it challenging to do so properly. They fail to recognize the highly complex linguistic codes and rules one must know before being able to speak it with fluency—that is, in a way that teachers view as substandard! I make this point to stress that the brilliance of neoindigenous youth cannot be appreciated by educators who are conditioned to perceive anything outside their own ways of knowing and being as not having value. This is similar to white teachers at the Carlisle School who sought to ban the language and customs of their indigenous students and replace them with "American culture." The University of Minnesota Human Rights Center describes this process as the silencing of voice and history that is part of the indigenous experience. I argue that enduring this silencing process is something that both the indigenous and neoindigenous have in common, and should be used as a way to connect them.

Though there are obvious historical differences between the neoindigenous and the indigenous, it is important to recognize that urban youth are working within what Maori indigenous professor Manuhuia Barcham describes as the "politics of indigeneity,"[9] which reinforces power structures that privilege certain voices while silencing and attempting to erase the history and value of others.

Consider, for example, the denial of the genocide of Aboriginal Australians by former prime minister John Howard despite reports and testimonials that confirmed the horrors they endured. This same denial exists today with neoindigenous populations who are pushed out of schools and into prisons and who can clearly articulate the personal devaluation they undergo in urban public schools. On a re-cent visit to a prison where I was speaking to young men of color who had been incarcerated for anywhere from two to twenty years, I struck up a conversation with a group of young men who described a number of incidents in their respective public schools that caused them to doubt whether or not school was for them. One story in particular resonated with me because of how similar it was to conver-sations I've had with other former urban public school students who have spent their lives doubting their own intelligence and making life decisions about what they can or cannot do based on something a teacher told them. This young man shared with me his experience in middle school, when a science teacher told him he was wasting his time going to school because all he would be when he got older was a gangbanger. He described this event and the older white male teacher in such detail, it was clear he had carried the incident with him for decades. I've heard versions of this story in rap songs, class-rooms, prisons, and homeless shelters countless times. Despite its prominence, however, it is not part of the existent discourse on ur-ban teaching and learning. When I mention it in academic circles, I am always challenged to think about it as the exception and not the norm. This denial of my reality in academic spaces signals more than individual denials of others' histories; it is a systemic denial within institutions built upon white cultural traditions that oppress and si-lence the indigenous and the neoindigenous.

When the indigenous and neoindigenous are silenced, they tend to respond to the denial of their voices by showcasing their culture in vivid, visceral, and transgressive ways. For Aboriginal populations, the *corroboree* is an event that transforms contemporary contexts via costume, music, dance, and ritual enactments. These celebrations enable participants to make a powerful political statement about how they are positioned in society and the importance of reclaiming their voices. These expressions of self are framed as entertainment or spectacles to be observed by tourists, as well as members of the dominant culture. As such they are an embodiment of what it means to be indigenous.

Like the indigenous, urban youth distinguish themselves from the larger culture through their dress, their music, their creativity in nonacademic endeavors, and their artistic output. In much public discourse, the ways in which they express themselves creatively are denigrated. For example, as a form of neoindigenous music, hip-hop is often dismissed by traditional cultural critics as "vulgar." The innovation and technical skill required to create and perform this music is secondary to its "message," which is often seen as threatening to mainstream culture and out of step with its values. Indeed, record companies deemphasize the music's "message" to white audiences, while pushing the dance moves and style of dress of hip-hop artists to market this music.

Like the indigenous, who have been relegated to certain geographic areas with little resources but still find a way to maintain their traditions, the neoindigenous in urban areas have developed ways to live within socioeconomically disadvantaged spaces while maintaining their dignity and identity. They are blamed for achievement gaps, neighborhood crime, and high incarceration rates, while the system that perpetuates these issues remains unchallenged. In urban schools, where the neoindigenous are taught to be docile and complicit in their own miseducation and then celebrated for being everything but who they are, they learn quickly that they are expected to divorce themselves from their culture in order to be academically successful. For many youth, this process involves the loss of their dignity and a shattering of their personhood. Urban youth who enter schools seeing themselves as smart and capable are confronted by curriculum that is blind to their realities and school rules that seek to erase their culture. These youth, because they do not have the space/opportunity to showcase their worth on their own terms in schools, are only visible when they enact very specific behaviors. This usually means they have the focus of the teacher only when they are being loud and verbal (often read by educators as disruptive), or silent and compliant (often read by educators as well behaved). Educators are trained to perceive any expression of neoindigenous culture (which is often descriptive and verbal) as inherently negative and will only view the students positively when they learn to express their intelligence in ways that do not reflect their neoindigeneity. Students quickly receive the message that they can only be smart when they are not who they are. This, in many ways, is classroom colonialism; and it can only be addressed through a very different approach to teaching and learning.

I do not engage in the work of connecting indigenous and neoindigenous either to trivialize the indigenous experience or exaggerate that of the neoindigenous. My point is to identify and acknowledge the collective oppression both groups experience and the shared space they inhabit as a result of their authentic selves being deemed invisible. Indeed, customs of the Maori in New Zealand vary as much from those of Indigenous Americans as urban youth from Los Angeles differ from their counterparts in New York City. However, their similarities are glowingly apparent if we choose to focus on them, and they offer a powerful new framework for urban education. The indigenous and neoindigenous are groups that have been victimized by different forms of the same oppression. The Bronx, New York, has no privilege over Gary, Indiana, just as Aboriginal voices have no value over the African indigenous. George Dei and Alireza Asgharzadeh, who have done powerful research on indigenous knowledge and postcolonial thought, argue that oppression "differentiates individuals and communities from one another" but "at the same time connects them to each other through the experience of being oppressed, marginalized, and colonized."[10] This is the reason I connect the indigenous and neoindigenous.

Indigenous and diasporic scholars have consistently argued that the ways we view those we consider "indigenous" must move beyond prescribed definitions issuing from colonial and imperial constructs and toward a more inclusive definition that considers how people categorize themselves based on their shared experiences with imperialism and colonialism in their varied forms.[11] This definition allows us to see how the indigenous exist across diverse places yet remain connected. For example, the Aboriginal, the Maori, and the Indigenous American experience colonization and/or imperialism in different ways across different contexts but each group underperforms when compared to their white counterparts.[12] These same achievement gaps exist between neoindigenous urban youth of color and their counterparts from majority-white schools with students of middle to high socioeconomic status.

Given the extended analogies between the indigenous and neoindigenous described above, and the ways that I have both experientially and theoretically showcased the connections between the two, it is clear that many teachers in urban schools today share the misguided, though caring, impulse that maintained poor schooling at the Carlisle School. The work for white folks who teach in urban schools, then, is to unpack their privileges and excavate the institutional, societal, and personal histories they bring with them when they come to the hood.

In this work, the term *white folks* is an obvious racial classification, but it also identifies a group that is associated with power and the use of power to disempower others. My use of the term *white folks* draws from the short story collection *The Ways of White Folks*, by Langston Hughes.[13] These stories revolve around interactions between white and black people that can only be described as unfortunate cultural clashes. These clashes occur when the world of one group does not seamlessly merge with that of another group because of a fundamental difference in the ways they are positioned in the world. In each story, the black characters interact with white characters, ranging from the innocuous to the outrightly racist, with negative outcomes for the black characters. Hughes was deliberate in not painting all white people with a broad brush. He even has one of his characters mention "the ways of white folks, I mean some white folks." Despite this effort, Hughes constructs a context where the societally sanctioned power that white people have over black people results in drama, and some humor, but overall outcomes that are largely unfavorable for the black characters.

Drawing from Hughes's framing, I am not painting all white teachers as being the same. In fact, there are some people of color who engage in what Hughes would call "the ways of white folks."

However, there are power dynamics, personal histories, and cultural clashes stemming from whiteness and all it encompasses that work against young people of color in traditional urban classrooms. This book highlights them, provides a framework for looking at them, and offers ways to address them in the course of improving the education of urban youth of color.

CHAPTER 1

Camaraderie

Reality and the Neoindigenous

I am a man of substance, of flesh and bone, fiber and liquids—and I might even be said to possess a mind. I am invisible, understand, simply because people refuse to see me. Like the bodiless heads you see sometimes in circus sideshows, it is as though I have been surrounded by mirrors of hard, distorting glass. When they approach me they see only my surroundings, themselves, or figments of their imagination—indeed, everything and anything except me.

—RALPH ELLISON

Ralph Ellison's *Invisible Man* describes the complexities of blackness in America and captures the ways that the segregated South and its ugly history of racism had inscribed itself so indelibly into the psyche of the "more accepting" and progressive North in the 1950s that it rendered African Americans invisible. The book's protagonist is so shaped by the conditions of his time that he becomes a distorted version of himself, his "true self" rendered invisible. This haunting and powerful story resonates with the experiences of urban youth in today's urban classrooms. The poet Adrienne Rich affirmed this sense of negation when she observed that "when someone with the authority of a teacher, say, describes the world and you are not in it, there is a moment of psychic disequilibrium, as if you looked in the mirror and saw nothing."[1]

Consider a common scenario in urban schools, and one I have witnessed often, where the teacher and student have different conceptions about what it means to be on time and prepared for class. For many students, being on time and prepared means being in or around the physical space of the classroom at the appointed hour and being able to access whatever materials are necessary for the day's instruction. This runs counter to a more narrowly defined, traditional perception of being prepared for learning, and can result in students being made invisible to the teacher. I experienced a perfect example of this "making invisible" process during a pre-suspension meeting for a student whose science teacher had accused her of being disruptive, unprepared for class, and habitually tardy. As the teacher began to describe the reasons for the suspension, the student stood up and said, "That's not true, that's just not true." Calmly, the principal asked the student to stop being disrespectful. The student looked bewildered and sat down with tears streaming down her face, biting at her thumb, her knee shaking so forcefully I thought she might knock the principal's desk over. At the end of the meeting, she snatched the pink sheet of paper that described the procedures for her two-day suspension and stormed out of the office. Her teacher seemed frozen to her seat as the scenario played out, unsure of what to do next.

A few minutes later, having heard the teacher's litany of complaints that had led to the student's suspension, I walked through the school building and spotted the student in the middle of a crowd of friends. They had rallied around her and seemed to be consoling her. When I asked her if we could talk, she looked up reluctantly and slowly walked toward me. As she did so, a bell rang signaling the change of classroom periods. The students who had gathered around their friend quickly dispersed, heading to their respective classrooms. I noticed that a significant number of them stood at the doors of the classrooms or lingered between the doorways, shouting greetings to their friends who were passing by. As we walked the hallway, she pointed to a friend who pointed back at her, then asked me, "Is *he* late? Is *he* unprepared for class?" She then motioned to another friend who was straddling the doorway to a class and asked, "Is *she* late? Is *she* distracting the class?" I didn't quite know how to respond and so I didn't. She took that to mean that I understood her. "Exactly," she said. "I'm always ready for that lady's class and she gets me sus-pended because she doesn't know what she's doing. She sees what she wants to see." As we talked more, I mentioned that the teacher said she never had her books with her for class. She responded that a friend shares her books with her and lends her something to write with whenever she needs it. For her, that made it obvious that she was prepared to learn. She then mentioned that she was always on time for class. "I'm always at the door when that bell rings. I'm al-ways there." The student saw herself as prepared and on time, but the teacher did not see the student the way she saw herself.

The point here is not to debate whether the teacher or the stu-dent was right or wrong; there isn't a clear answer to that question. What's important to note is that the teacher in this scenario had rendered the student's self-image as "prepared and on time" invisible. That image had been replaced with one in which the student was seen as disruptive, chronically late, and unprepared, a distortion of the student's self-image. This was the case even though the student mentioned that she liked the subject being taught and was excited about what she was learning in her science class. This teacher, who struggled to get her students engaged in science, had alienated one of the few students who liked the class, because she did not fit the mold the school and the teacher had cast for what a good student looks and acts like.

The reality is that we privilege people who look and act like us, and perceive those who don't as different and, frequently, inferior. In urban schools, and especially for those who haven't had previous experience in urban contexts or with youth of color, educators learn "best practices" from "experts" in the field, deemed as such because they have degrees, write articles, and meet other criteria that do not have anything to do with their work within urban communities. In fact, many of us who think about the education of youth of color have developed our ideas about the field from specialists who can describe the broad landscape of urban education but are often far removed, both geographically and psychologically, from the schools and students that they speak and write about so eloquently.

Urban education experts typically don't live in urban communities. They don't look like the students they discuss in meetings and conferences, and when they do, they often make class distinctions that separate them from students. Most importantly, they don't consider their distance from these communities as an impediment to their ability to engage in the work within them. The leaders within the field of urban education can't fathom the day-to-day experiences of urban students who see themselves as ready to learn despite not being perceived that way. They don't see the deep connections that exist between urban experience and school performance; many more have come to view school as a discrete space, as if what happens outside school has little to no impact on what happens inside school. This discourse among "experts" (politicians, professors, media pundits) has made it okay for teachers to work within urban communities they either refuse to live in or are afraid to live in. The nature of how we view urban-education expertise has created a context that dismisses students' lives and experiences while concurrently speaking about, and advocating for, equity and improving schools. Consider, for example, the growing number of new charter schools in urban communities with words like *success*, *reform*, and *equity* in their names and mission statements, but which engage in teaching practices that focus on making the school and the students within it as separate from the community as possible.

I engaged in a Twitter debate with one of these educators recently and was astounded by the fervor with which he defended his school's practice of "cleaning these kids up and giving them a better life." With that statement, he described everything that is wrong with the culture of urban education and the biggest hindrance to white folks who teach in the hood. First, the belief that students are in need of "cleaning up" presumes that they are dirty. Second, the aim of "giving them a better life" indicates that their present life has little or no value. The idea that one individual or school can give students "a life" emanates from a problematic savior complex that results in making students, their varied experiences, their emotions, and the good in their communities invisible. So invisible, in fact, that the chief way to teach urban youth of color more effectively—that is, to truly be in and in touch with their communities—is not seen as a viable option.

Physical Place and Emotional Space

To be in touch with the community, one has to enter into the physical places where the students live, and work to be invited into the emotion-laden spaces the youth inhabit. The places may be housing projects or overcrowded apartment buildings, but the spaces are what philosopher Kelly Oliver describes as psychic.[2] They are filled with emotions like fear, anger, and a shared alienation from the norms of school, birthed from experiences both within and outside the school building. The places transcend geography and are more about what is felt by being in a particular location.

The urban youth who inhabit these complex psychic spaces, and for whom imagination is the chief escape from harsh realities, walk through life wrapped in a shroud of emotions whose fibers are their varied daily experiences. The gunshot that rang past an apartment window (the experience) and the fear and anxiety that resulted from it (the emotion) creates a reality that is almost impossible for an outsider to fully comprehend. I remember being a tenth-grade student who attended a large comprehensive "specialized" urban public school. I took the train for an hour each day because the school I attended was better than the local ones in my neighborhood. One evening after a long day and what seemed like an equally long train ride home, I walked into my apartment building, and just as the large metal door closed behind me gunshots rang out just outside the door. I froze for a second, not knowing where the shots were coming from, when my younger sister, tugging at my arm, pulled me through the interior door of our apartment building as the shots continued to ring behind me. When I got into my family's apartment that night, and my sister described what had happened to my mother, she told me that I couldn't afford to freeze up in moments like that. I was told to be alert and drop to the floor at the sound of gunfire.

About a week later, I sat in my mathematics class as the teacher droned on about how to solve an equation. The class was silent except for the scratching of chalk against the blackboard as the teacher worked on the problem. A chair held the door open to let air into the classroom, but it wasn't enough to alleviate the stifling atmosphere in the boring class. As the teacher continued to write, a loud noise suddenly erupted from out in the hallway. Before I could even think, I jumped out of my seat and underneath my desk. I cowered on the floor for what seemed like forever until I heard my entire class break out in roaring laughter. I emerged from underneath the desk to find my teacher standing in the aisle and another student admonishing me for trying to be the class clown. The teacher's left hand hit my desk with a light thud and his right one pointed toward the door as the words "Principal's office, now" rolled from his lips. The class continued laughing as I grabbed my books and headed toward the door. In that moment, I couldn't find the words to explain that the loud sound I had heard reminded me of the shootout that I had barely missed getting caught in a week ago. There was no way to describe that the trauma of my experience the previous week was what caused me to jump under the desk in fear for my life. There was no way that the teacher or the principal could ever understand what I was feeling in that moment unless they had experienced it, and so I coolly grabbed my jacket and books, put on a smile for my friends, winked at the teacher, and walked out of the classroom.

Much research has been done on post-traumatic stress disorder and its impact on those afflicted. We tend to associate PTSD with combat veterans, but too often we fail to recognize that young people experience trauma regularly in ways that go unnoticed or unrecognized. For example, a study I conducted with black males who had either attended or were presently enrolled in urban public schools revealed symptoms of PTSD among participants. My coresearcher on the project, PTSD specialist and psychologist Napoleon Wells, identified the students' avoidance of certain discussions and reactions to others as similar to the ways that veterans respond after exposure to trauma. In fact, the students' symptoms of fear, anger, and powerlessness led to what Dr. Wells calls postracial tension stress disorder, which derives from youth seeing themselves as powerless in a world that conveys to them the message that race doesn't matter, at the same time it subjects them to physical and symbolic violence (at the hands of police and schools) because of their race.

In schools, urban youth are expected to leave their day-to-day experiences and emotions at the door and assimilate into the culture of schools. This process of personal repression is in itself traumatic and directly impacts what happens in the classroom. Students exist in a space within the classroom while the teacher limits their understanding to what is happening in the classroom place. Failure to prepare teachers to appreciate the psychic spaces students occupy inevitably limits their effectiveness. Some teachers understand that students come from places beyond the classroom and can acknowledge that these places have an effect on students and the spaces they occupy. However, many teachers cannot see beyond their immediate location (the school) and therefore have a very limited understanding of space. Many more are taught to ignore psychic space altogether, and therefore cannot fathom what it must be like for students to whom the classroom is a breeding ground for traumatic experiences. Once again, these students are unseen by teachers, mere reflections of teachers' perceptions of who they are. This is what Ellison described as people not seeing him but "surroundings, themselves, or figments of their imagination—indeed, everything and anything except me."[3]

The work to become truly effective educators in urban schools requires a new approach to teaching that embraces the complexity of place, space, and their collective impact on the psyche of urban youth. This approach is necessary whether we are talking about preservice educators about to embark on their first year of teaching, those who have been in the field for a while, or the millions of people who have been drawn into the dysfunctional web of urban education as a parent, policymaker, or concerned citizen. Addressing the issues that plague urban education requires a true vision that begins with seeing students in the same way they see themselves.

Urban youth are typically well aware of the loss, pain, and injustice they experience, but are ill equipped for helping each other through the work of navigating who they truly are and who they are expected to be in a particular place. At seventeen years old, Youth Poet Laureate of the City of Oakland, California, Obasi Davis wrote the poem "Bored in 1st Period." Obasi, who is now a college student in a predominantly white institution of higher education, wrote this piece as a high school student seeing peers who are rendered invisible by their school and teachers even as he could see their true selves in plain view. In the excerpts of the poem reprinted below, the reader can see his deep analysis of his peers and the difference between who they are in the classroom (place) and who they truly are within a shared emotional space.

BORED IN 1ST PERIOD
Asia comes from repossessed dreams and nightmares that last as
long as the absence of her father
> *I think that's the reason her clothes are always so Boa*
> *Constricting any amount of longing she might have felt for him*
> *to me*
Daniel spent his childhood running from Richmond bullets and the
ghost of his dad
> *Daniel is a* thug
He brags about seeing grown men ground to dust under heavy
boots for their iPhones and their wallets
> *He rocks a long gold chain, a grill, and two diamond*
>> *earrings with*
> *every outfit*
> *Daniel only cares about money*
> *but I can see genius bursting from his pained skin*
> *It is the deepest black, pure like Earth's blood*
> *but for some reason, most seem to see it as an*
> impurity.
> *He paints himself a gangster to cover what they call ugly*
Jonathan chooses to come to class once a month or whenever we

have a sub

He shoots dice in the back corner of the classroom with Duma
     and Daniel

When I ask them why, they tell me money is everything.

It seems they are the products of a broken society and a torn home

My home is not broken

My parents are divorced but they get along

I haven't known death to come close,

and violence hasn't found me vulnerable

And then, while sitting in 1st period pretending to read Macbeth,
     it clicked for me

My classmates and I are different

In the words of Dr. King our elbows are together yet our
     hearts are

apart

I'm not asking for some all holy savior to come and coddle us
into equality

I'm asking for you to understand our struggles and our hardships

To understand that if we have to learn with each other we should also
learn about each other so we can bring each other up

What Obasi describes in this poem is a reality that many who interact with students on a daily basis will never see. He describes students in a classroom (place) who exist in worlds/spaces wholly distinct from the classroom. He shows us that what educators and the world at large see when looking at students is often a distortion of their authentic selves. Furthermore, he alludes to the major premise of this work—that what lies beyond what we see are deep stories, complex connections, and realities that factors like race, class, power, and the beliefs/presuppositions educators hold inhibit them from seeing. Teaching to who students are requires a recognition of their realities.

John Searle defines reality as an agreed-upon outlook on or about social life based on how it is perceived or created by a group of people. He also sees reality as "facts relative to a system of values that we hold."[4] This definition provides a simple yet necessary framework for understanding youth realities—because it moves educators to focus on the ways that youth see the world and their position in it based on the facts, laws, rules, and principles that govern the places they are from and the consequent spaces they inhabit. This provides the educator with a very different vantage point for seeing them and gives information about place while providing insight into emotional space.

In order to fully understand youth realities, and make some sense of the powerful connection between youth realities, place, and space, I argue that educators need a new lens and vocabulary. This is why I argue for making connections between urban youth, or the neoindigenous, and the indigenous. While the word *neoindigeneity* may appear to the reader as yet another loaded academic term that has no significance in real urban classrooms, it is far from that. I use this term throughout this work as a way to make sense of the realities of the urban youth experience. Framing urban youth as neoindigenous, and understanding that the urban youth experience is deeply connected to the indigenous experience, provides teachers with a very different worldview when working with youth. From this new vantage point, teachers can see, access, and utilize tools for teaching urban youth. An understanding of neoindigineity allows educators to go beyond what they physically see when working with urban youth, and attend to the relationship between place and space.

For the indigenous, the relationship to emotional space is a constitutive part of their existence. For these populations, when one is hurt, healing requires addressing both physical wounds and the "soul wounds." Healing the physical wound occurs in a certain place, but healing the soul wound requires being in a space. The psychologist Eduardo Duran states that counseling Native Americans and other indigenous people requires entering into the spaces in which they reside, because as Mark Findlay identifies, there are understandings that cannot be visible within the institutions (places) of the power wielder.[5] This type of healing work is necessary for the neoindigenous as well. Situations such as the suspension of the student who believed she was prepared for class and always on time result in soul wounds that are bigger than the disciplinary issue itself and could be avoided if the teacher validated the student's emotion by allowing her to articulate her feelings. Recognizing the neoindigeneity of youth requires acknowledgement of the soul wounds that teaching practices inflict upon them.

If we are truly interested in transforming schools and meeting the needs of urban youth of color who are the most disenfranchised within them, educators must create safe and trusting environments that are respectful of students' culture. Teaching the neoindigenous requires recognition of the spaces in which they reside, and an understanding of how to see, enter into, and draw from these spaces. In the chapters that follow, I describe how educators may engage in this healing process through an approach to teaching I call reality pedagogy.

Reality Pedagogy

Reality pedagogy is an approach to teaching and learning that has a primary goal of meeting each student on his or her own cultural and emotional turf. It focuses on making the local experiences of the student visible and creating contexts where there is a role reversal of sorts that positions the student as the expert in his or her own teaching and learning, and the teacher as the learner. It posits that while the teacher is the person charged with delivering the content, the student is the person who shapes how best to teach that content. Together, the teacher and students co-construct the classroom space.

Reality pedagogy allows for youth to reveal how and where teaching and learning practices have wounded them. The approach works toward making students wholly visible to each other and to the teacher and focuses on open discourse about where students are academically, psychologically, and emotionally. In a reality-pedagogy-based classroom, every individual is perceived as having a distinct perspective and is given the opportunity to express that in the classroom. There is no grand narrative. Instead of seeing the students as equal to their cultural identity, a reality pedagogue sees students as individuals who are influenced by their cultural identity. This means that the teacher does not see his or her classroom as a group of African American, Latino, or poor students and therefore does not make assumptions about their interests based on those preconceptions. Instead, the teacher begins from an understanding of the students as unique individuals and then develops approaches to teaching and learning that work for those individuals. This approach acknowledges the preconceptions, guilt, and biases a white teacher in a predominantly African American or Latino urban school may bring to the classroom because it considers the history of teaching and learning in contexts like the Carlisle School and consciously avoids replicating them.

In preparing teachers to teach in urban schools, I often show still images of students from classroom videos that I have collected over the last decade. The students in the images range in age from six to twenty-one and are all students of color from urban schools across the country. Each image shows students in varying poses of what could be described as disinterest. They range from heads rested on classroom desks or on palms that seem to be holding up much more than weary heads to students looking at the teacher with blank, emotionless stares. In one exercise, these images were presented to the teachers in whose classrooms the pictures were taken, and the teachers were asked to describe the students' realities. I would ask teachers to look at the images and describe what was going through each student's mind at the moment when his or her picture was taken. The responses from the teachers were quite similar and along the lines of "He doesn't want to be there" and "She is bored or angry." After this process, I provided teachers with transcripts from interviews with the students photographed, in which the students described what they were thinking and feeling at the moment their images were captured. Once this happened, the huge gap between how students experienced the world and how teachers viewed this same world became evident.

In one scenario, during a professional-development session where a large number of teachers from an urban school district gathered on a cold November afternoon, two images of an African American young man from a classroom in one of their schools were projected onto a screen. In one image, he is staring emptily into space, and in the other, his head is resting on his desk. Responses from the group were immediate, and all described the young man in the photos as some variation of "disinterested" or "unmotivated." I then hit the button on my laptop that played the video of the moments before and after the two images were taken. In the video, the young man tries repeatedly to answer a question that the teacher had posed. He raises his hand, stares at the teacher to get his attention, and even yells out the answer after he is initially ignored. After multiple futile attempts to be recognized by the teacher, he puts his head down on the desk.

When I interviewed this student after I had seen the video, he revealed a deep desire to learn and an undeniable frustration with the fact that the structures in place in the classroom, like his seat being at the back of the class, the pace of the lesson being too slow, and the students not having the space to discuss the content with each other, wouldn't allow this desire to be met. He mentioned that he put his head on the desk in an attempt to control the anger and frustration that came from not being validated and not being taught well. He knew that if he responded angrily, he would be perceived as "mad for no reason" and probably "kicked out of the class or suspended like they usually do when you say something." In this scenario, the different ways that teachers experienced the student's reaction to the classroom highlights the need for understanding the authentic realities of young people. A conversation with the teacher about this video revealed that, according to the teacher, the student had to learn to control his excitement and had not shown that he was ready to learn. In this scenario both the teacher and the student are experiencing the same classroom in very different ways.

Addressing the tensions that come out of these two authentic yet very different realities requires an approach to teaching and learning that functions to bridge the differences in experience within the classroom while allowing the teacher and student to co-construct a learning space that meets their unique needs. Reality pedagogy focuses on privileging the ways that students make sense of the classroom while acknowledging that the teacher often has very different expectations about the classroom. This approach to teaching focuses on the subtleties of teaching and learning that are traditionally glossed over by teachers and administrators while addressing the nuances of teaching that are not part of teacher-education programs and crash courses that lead to teacher certification. Reality pedagogy considers the range of emotions that new teachers experience when embarking on their careers but also acknowledges the experiences that veteran teachers may have had that left them jaded. Most importantly, it begins with the acceptance of the often overlooked fact that there are cultural differences between students and their teachers that make it difficult for teachers to be reflective and effective, while providing a set of steps that allow these misalignments to be overcome.

Reality pedagogy does not draw its cues for teaching from "classroom experts" who are far removed from real schools, or from researchers who make suggestions for the best ways to teach "urban," "suburban," and "rural" youth based on their perceptions of what makes sense for classrooms. Rather, it focuses on teaching and learning as it is successfully practiced within communities physically outside of, and oftentimes beyond, the school. Rather than give teachers a set of tools to implement and hope that these approaches meet the specific needs of urban youth and their teachers in particular classrooms, reality pedagogy provides educators with a mechanism for developing approaches to teaching that meet the specific needs of the students sitting in front of them. In the chapters that follow, we will delve into this approach and outline how it serves as a way for white folks who teach in the hood—and the rest of y'all too—to improve their pedagogy.

CHAPTER 2

Courage
Teach Without Fear

On my first day as a teacher, after the principal led me and three other beginning teachers on a final tour of the school, I joined the rest of the faculty in the auditorium, preparing for the students to arrive. As we waited for the doors to open, the other new teachers and I struggled to mask the emotions that roiled beneath our calm facades. At one point, we peered between the bars on the windows of the auditorium to catch a glimpse of the students who were lined up against a graffiti-stained wall outside the school building. There they stood, in their first-day-of-school outfits: brand-new gleaming sneakers in an array of bright colors and perfectly coordinated clothes, experiencing a bevy of emotions themselves, poised to meet their new teachers.

A few feet from the auditorium, metal detectors adorned the big metal doors that the students would soon walk through. As the queue outside the door grew, so did the sound of the students' voices, and with them, the tension inside the room as the huge clock on the auditorium wall slowly ticked to 8:30. A fellow new teacher, impeccably dressed in the principal's recommended khakis and blazer, looked up at me. "Do you hear them out there?" she asked nervously as the school doors opened and the students began to stream in.

I responded to her question with a half-smile and shrug, intended to show that I wasn't intimidated. On the inside, it was a different story. I had heard about how tough these "urban kids" were going to be. At one point, I realized that my nervousness was evident as I observed my hand tremble; I quickly slipped it into my pocket. The fact that I had lived in neighborhoods just like the one in which the school stood, and may have walked past these students hundreds of times as I strode up and down these same streets, did nothing to calm my nerves. Somehow, the stories about angry and violent urban youth who did not want to be in school and did not want to learn stripped them of their humanity, erasing the reality that they were just children on the first day of school.

Fear-Based Narratives

The stereotypes we brought with us into that school auditorium shaped our understandings not only of the students we would be teaching but also of what it means to teach. Rather than approach teaching with the confidence that comes from knowing your mission and the joy of being placed in a school where one can fulfill it, we approached the arrival of the students with an unhealthy apprehension about what the next academic year would bring. We hyper-analyzed everything the students brought to the school in search of anything that would affirm the negative stories we had heard about them. Before they even spoke, we read their exchanges with each other and marked them as either teachable or not. We gave each other knowing glances based on how students walked through the auditorium. We would breathe a collective sigh of relief when a student appeared to be "teachable," and nod knowingly when a student looked like trouble. The seemingly shy and demure students, by virtue of not being the prototypical urban student described to us by the media and in popular narratives, became the teachable ones. These students elicited smiles and positive emotions. On the other hand, the students who spoke too loudly and seemed to be exuding too much confidence or "urbanness" were immediately judged "problem students."

The process of identifying the good and bad students became a game of sorts for me and the other new teachers. What we didn't realize as we began to play this game was that our seemingly impromptu categorizations of young people came from very real ideas about youth that we had subconsciously ingested. As we got deeper into this game, its complexity slowly revealed itself. The more my peers and I became preoccupied with positioning students as teachable or not, the more invested we became in the process. Our everyday conversations in our first year of teaching became reaffirmations of the categorizations we had developed on the first day. We were in many ways no different than European settlers in their first interactions with the indigenous, sharing observations of their unrefined culture and violent nature. We spent our lunch meetings and after-school professional-development sessions trying to one-up each other with stories about how challenging our students were. We spent so much time and energy exaggerating these stories that we became distracted from our initial goal to affect change. Our preoccupation with positioning ourselves as good guys in a war against the young people meant that we were fulfilling our chief function as cogs in the urban-education machine. The more we told tales of dysfunction, the more we worked to maintain it. This process eroded the unbridled passion that brought us into the field of education, transforming us into agents of a traditional school culture that worked against young people.

The process was subtle and took different forms for each of the teachers who stood in the auditorium that morning. For many of the white teachers, the process held an unmistakable element of racism. Phrases like "these kids" or "those kids" were often clearly code words for bad black and brown children.

The teachers' venting sessions reminded me of my experiences in high school and how I was forced to obey rules without an opportunity to question whether they supported the way I learned. As a high school student, the more I engaged in school, the more I learned about the rules that guided the institution and realized that they ran counter to the ways I experienced the world. The more I realized that there was a gap between who I was as a young black man and who the institution and the teachers wanted me to be, the more I rebelled against school and all it represented. In many ways, this is where the association between being academically successful and "acting white," studied by education researchers like John Ogbu, comes from.[1] These scholars argue that black youth view doing well in school as acting white, without considering that teachers may perceive being black as not wanting to do well in school. The issue is not that youth of color see academic success as limited to whites. It is that they typically see white teachers as enforcers of rules that are unrelated to the actual teaching and learning process. Consequently, they respond negatively to whatever structures these teachers value even at the expense of their own academic success.

In my experiences in school, I underperformed in classes in which teachers privileged ways of engaging with content that stifled my creativity and did well in classes where I wasn't forced to obey rules, but had an opportunity to learn. By my final year of high school, I had been identified as a troublemaker even though I wanted to go to college. Once I left high school, and with the constant reminder and awareness that I needed an education in order to be successful in the future, I learned to assimilate into the culture of traditional schooling. Unfortunately, this process meant that I spent almost all of my time in my final year of high school working to erase my everyday realities and dismiss the knowledge that I gained in my out-of-school world. The process of indoctrination was difficult, and I often rebelled against it. On occasion, when the work of conforming got too taxing, I would ask teachers questions to challenge the structures they had in place in the hope of improving the classroom environment. However, questions like, "Can we stand up and stretch if we need to?" were met with firm requests to sit back down and looks from the teacher that said much more about what the teachers thought of me than any words could. In response, I would take the bathroom pass and walk the hallways, thinking that I had won a game of sorts with the teacher. I got a chance to walk around and stretch and there was nothing that could be done about it. Unbeknownst to me, I was the loser in a larger game, missing out on what was being taught in the classroom and drawn into another game of cat and mouse with security officials who patrolled the building in search of students like me who were leaving class out of boredom, frustration, or just a chance to breathe. Either way, all of us who left our classrooms in silent protest against the oppressive structure of the classroom came to a point where we considered whether or not it was easier to sit in class and play the game of attentive student or challenge the rules that were being enforced by the teachers. A few decided to play the game, but many more either did not, or could not. The ones who played graduated high school, went on to college, and some even became teachers.

Years later, when I became a teacher, I learned much about the structure of urban schools and grew to become the embodiment of the very teachers who placed me in the vice that had squeezed all of the fight out of me as a student. Then, as I'd navigated the landscape of formal education and played a game whose rules were enforced largely by white folks who teach in the hood, I became conditioned to be a "proper student" and began to lose value for pieces of myself that previously defined me. My unabashed urbanness—loud, conspicuous, and questioning of authority—became lost. This was encouraged when I got into the teaching profession. When I took my first job in a school with students whose faces looked much like mine, the most memorable advice I received from an older teacher was, "You look too much like them, and they won't take you seriously. Hold your ground, and don't smile till November." To be an effective black male educator for youth of color, I was being advised to erase pieces of myself and render significant pieces of who I was invisible. That's what was needed to enter into teaching, which was increasingly being presented as a war against young people.

For my closest teacher colleague who stood in the auditorium with me when we began our careers, recruitment into the army against urban youth began when, as a young person, she was taught to "be a good person" and "leave a mark on the world." She was white and from a middle-class background and had seen pictures of her parents when they were in their twenties feeding poor children in Africa on missionary trips. She was chosen to teach in the school based on her good grades and "change the world" attitude as identified by a teacher-recruitment program that brought white folks to teach in the hood. A recent college graduate from a private liberal arts university, she was inspired by the idea of giving back to poor communities. She took the job to get the free master's degree that many new urban teachers receive, but was drawn into the profession by the opportunity to experience some version of her parents' missionary trips. The exotic images from her parents' photographs could be played out in her life through urban America, and her privilege had created a guilt that could be eased by teaching the poor black and brown kids in her classroom.

In our conversations, we explored our experiences on the path to becoming urban educators, discussed our motivations for teaching, our experiences thus far, and finally, the advice we had received to prepare us to successfully do the work we both believed we were called to do. I had been trained my entire life to believe that being something other than who I truly was would make me a better person. She had been trained to be herself and help the "less fortunate." Though our motivations and experiences were different, in the course of our conversations we learned that we had one thing in common: the constant reminder by peers, family members, teachers, and now school administrators to see urban youth of color as a group that is potentially dangerous and needs to be saved from themselves. We were both told not to express too much emotion with students or be too friendly with them. I was told to "stand your ground when they test you," "don't let them know anything about your life so they don't get too familiar," and "remember that there is nothing wrong with being mean." Everyone from whom we solicited advice shared a variation of the phrase "Don't smile till November."

The phrase was simple and memorable, and easily took hold in the hearts and minds of both my new colleague and myself. It became our mantra. In tense and uncomfortable moments, when students raised their voices and threats were hurled our way, it gave us boldness and confidence. We would share the same knowing glances that helped us to categorize students as teachable or not on the first day to reaffirm our stances as no-nonsense educators. The phrase kept us standing when our knees wobbled in the school auditorium on our first day of teaching and made us confident past November. Unfortunately, this same mantra required us to remove all emotion from our teaching. It turned us from passionate educators into automatons who worked to maintain the school's structures and inequities. Rather than face our fears, the mantra helped us to mask them. And because being in touch with one's emotions is the key to moving from the classroom (place) to the spaces where the students are, our students were invisible to us.

Facing Fear: Before and Beyond November

To be an educator in America today means that your students' test scores, GPAs, and graduation rates are the primary measures of your effectiveness. Standardized exams drive everything from curriculum to teaching. As a result, many teachers believe that anything aside from teaching to the test will be detrimental to students and teachers alike. This makes it easy for some educators to ascribe to the "Don't smile till November" mantra. Teachers become adept at creating high-pressure classrooms focused more on testing than teaching. Teachers are reduced to test-prep machines.

White folks who teach in the hood are particularly prone to this sort of rote model. This is especially the case if they are convinced that having all students pass tests creates some form of equity. In these cases they are so married to a curriculum that is sold as the only path to passing the test that there is no willingness to deviate from it even if it is harming students. Furthermore, teaching to an exam and strictly following a curriculum makes it easier for these teachers to remain emotionally disconnected from students.

Consider a scenario where a group of teachers I was working with were expected to teach a unit on Europe during the semester. As I worked with the teachers to plan for the unit, one of them began telling the group about a European tour she took with her family when she was a teenager. As the teachers individually planned their lessons, she spoke enthusiastically about the trip and shared a lot of powerful and engaging stories that merged with the themes in the unit. As the planning session ended, the teachers thanked her for her stories and headed to their respective classes with the lessons they had worked on in tow.

Over the course of the next week, I visited a number of these teachers' classes and found all of their lessons to be similar. This was even the case when I went to the class of the teacher who had entertained us with her travel stories. None of her amazing stories had made it into her lesson. When I asked her why this was the case, she threw out a number of excuses that included not wanting to get too personal with her students, not wanting to be perceived as bragging, only having enough time in the lesson to cover what she was expected to, and wanting to follow the unit she was given by the school administration. Despite my efforts to convince the teacher that her personal stories could have helped her engage her students, she was adamant in her belief that sharing them would have undermined her in some way. This same teacher was one of many who later complained at the end of the academic year about how poorly students did on the standardized test she was so intent on teaching to.

In a related scenario, after working with a science teacher who complained incessantly that she needed glassware like beakers and pipettes in order to engage her students in science, I convinced the school administration to purchase these materials for her classes. Because funding for such an acquisition was a challenge, I actually bought some of the requested materials on my own. Eventually, after a few months, a number of lab materials were delivered to the teacher's classroom. I excitedly visited her classroom week after week to see what impact the new materials were having on science instruction, but a month went by and the materials still had not been put to use. Frustrated, I finally asked her what was up. After a long pause, she responded by saying that she'd had a change of heart and wasn't sure that the students were ready to use the items. She worried they might be used as weapons. What if the students broke the glass and used it to cut each other? Obviously, in constructing this narrative she was guided by her perception of her students as potentially violent. Unfortunately, their teacher's presuppositions had robbed these students of a promising learning opportunity.

In each of the scenarios described above, the white teachers held perceptions about the students and the type of instruction they needed that were rooted in bias. The notion that students wouldn't respond to powerful personal stories or would resort to violence if given the opportunity is clearly rooted in stereotypes about poverty, and in these cases black and brown youth of color. These biases were then used to justify ineffective teaching that is absolved from critique because of its supposed alignment to standardized exams. In reality, the persistence of achievement gaps proves that teaching that is not personalized and not hands-on (as is most teaching in traditional urban schools) does not equate to success on standardized exams. It also should lead to conversations about how these approaches to teaching actually support the persistence of the gaps they are designed to close.

When teaching doesn't connect to students, it is perceived as not belonging to them. Students begin to use phrases like "your exam" or "their test" when describing the assessments they are required to take, signaling to the educators that there is no vested interest in the test or their success on it. These same students exhibit resilience, dedication, and hard work in a number of tasks in their neighborhoods and devote hours on end to supporting each other in activities that have real meaning.

I remember one eighth-grade student I taught who had perfect attendance at school but whom I had identified as disconnected and disinterested in my class. I ran into her a few years later at a movie theater housed in a local shopping mall. When I recognized her from a few feet away, she tried to avoid eye contact with me and turned toward the concession stand. It was pretty obvious that she wasn't interested in reminiscing about old times. Taking the hint, I turned in the opposite direction and slowly attempted to make my way out of the theater. As I did so, one of the small children she had with her broke free and came running in my direction. My former student lunged after him and we ended up almost running into each other. I smiled and said hello, she did the same, and I bent over to introduce myself to the boy who was now clutching her leg while narrowly missing the swinging leg of the child she held in her arms. Her other hand clutching another child's hand, she introduced me to her son, little brother, and sister. I quickly calculated that she was now a junior in high school and asked her how school was going. She told me that she was the primary caregiver to her two younger siblings, since her mother had passed away during the year I was her teacher. She spoke to me about the declining health of her grandmother, whom she lived with, and of her decision to stay in school because she wanted to make something of her life. About her current high school experience, she then said, "All those white teachers be acting just like you, just meaner." In that moment, she uncovered how prevalent that "mean" style of teaching was, but also displayed her incredible resilience. I had perceived her as disconnected and disinterested in school, even though she was obviously the opposite of that. Unfortunately, I'd had no structures in place at the time to forge a connection with this student and allow her to tap into the resilience that brought her to school every day and help her apply it in my class.

I understand the pressures teachers are under and the challenges they face meeting high standards for success on measures that seem insurmountable. The current landscape of urban education, which holds teachers accountable for student outcomes while failing to equip teachers with the tools to meet these outcomes is paralyzing. However, the key to getting students to be academically successful (even if the teacher decides that success means passing an exam), is not to teach directly to the assessment or to the curriculum, but to teach *directly to the students*. Every educator who works with the neoindigenous must first recognize their students' neoindigeneity and teach from the standpoint of an ally who is working with them to reclaim their humanity.

To be an ally to the neoindigenous, the teacher must unpack the indoctrination that we have all been subject to. For white folks who teach in the hood, this may require a much more intense unpacking. For me, this meant taking the time to analyze why I was initially scared of my students and moving beyond that fear, acknowledging that getting to know my students and having them know me may alter the power structure and affect classroom management.

For many teachers, the school day has devolved into nothing more than a series of routines. If students are seated and quiet during most of the lesson, and teachers only have to yell enough times to get a sore throat once or twice a month, they view themselves as successful. They may not be reaching the students, or inspiring them to value education, but they rest comfortably knowing that they are doing their job as defined by the school. The lessons are scripted and the students are quiet. One group of students trickles in begrudgingly at the sound of the bell, and the same group pushes out of the class hastily at the sound of another bell. A dissenter among the group occasionally steps out of line and a referral is written or security is called. The pattern continues across classrooms throughout the day, and as long as there isn't an emergency, everything is perceived to be okay. This routine is familiar to many urban educators and allows them to maintain that things are not as bad as they could be rather than focus on how they should be. In this way, we become comfortable with dysfunctional teaching.

In my view, we do not see daily emergencies because we are conditioned to the norms of teaching and learning that are in themselves in a state of emergency. The entire system of urban education is failing youth of color by any number of criteria, the structure of the traditional urban school privileges poor teaching practices, these practices trigger responses from students that reflect "poor behavior," the poor behavior triggers deeply entrenched biases that teachers hold, and when this triggering of biases is coupled with the cycling in and out of white folks to teach in the hood, former teachers with activated biases leave urban classrooms to become policymakers and education experts who do not believe in young people or their communities. In response, I suggest an approach to urban education that benefits the two most significant parties in the traditional school—the student and the teacher—an approach to teaching and learning that not only considers what is right for students, but what makes the teacher most effective and fulfilled. This vision of teaching doesn't hide the fact that challenges in urban education persist because of our collective investment in maintaining a system that is intent on forcing brilliance to silence itself and then dealing with the varied repercussions. Once educators recognize that they are biased against forms of brilliance other than their own, they can finally begin to truly teach.

The new teachers I stood with in that auditorium on the first day of school, the teacher who failed to share with her students her stories about traveling in Europe, and the one who let fear stand in the way of providing her students with lab materials that would engage them in science—all of us had something in common. Our understandings of who was and wasn't a good student were rooted less in our experiences with urban students and more on our perceptions of them, which were largely based on a flawed narrative.

In my experience, having attended an urban public school and having taught in one years later, I found that not challenging the prevailing narrative about urban students led me to teach in ways that would not have worked for me when I was a student. If the teenage me had walked into the auditorium in which I stood on my first day as a teacher, the adult me would have judged my teenage self as unprepared for learning and not properly equipped for being intellectually challenged; from the way I looked and acted, I would have been labeled "trouble." On the path to becoming a teacher, I had learned to shed all elements of my teenage self. Not being able to smile till November robbed me of the opportunity of seeing myself in the students in front of me. Instead, the structures of schooling forced me to devalue anyone who brought any semblance of my teenage self into the present-day classroom. Today, with thousands of hours of teacher observations under my belt and having spent innumerable hours reflecting back on my own teaching, it is clear to me how teachers develop and maintain a deficit view of students. This is particularly evident when I think of how teachers of color have been taught to manage the behavior of students who do look like them, despite knowing that their neoindigeneity requires their voices being heard and their ideas validated.

The work for teachers becomes developing the self-reflection necessary to deconstruct the ways that media messages, other teachers' negative (often exaggerated) stories, and their own need to be the hero affects how they see and teach students. The teacher must work to ensure that the institution does not absolve them of the responsibility to acknowledge the baggage they bring to the classroom and analyze how that might affect student achievement. Without teachers recognizing the biases they hold and how these biases impact the ways they see and teach students, there is no starting point to changing the dismal statistics related to the academic underperformance of urban youth.

CHAPTER 3

Chuuuuch

Pentecostal Pedagogy

A solemn hymn played in the background as brilliant hues of auburn, gold, and blue flowed from the stained glass windows of a hundred-year-old church in Harlem. The light from the windows reflected off ornate wooden pews that formed two sets of parallel lines from the front of the cavernous room to the huge wooden doors at the back. The doors would swing open every few minutes as people entered, and the light from outside would stream across the pews, which shone so brightly they seemed to have been lacquered a million times. The glow of the pews contrasted with the dull maroon carpet that stretched from the doors at the back of the room to the elevated platform in front of it. On the platform, an organist, his eyes closed and his head swaying back and forth, provided a soundtrack of old Negro spirituals that summoned the well-dressed crowd from the streets of Harlem into the church. Older ladies with their grandchildren in their arms, gray-haired men in pristine suits, young men in bow ties, and young ladies in bright colored dresses made their way into the church and found a seat in the pews.

When the service was about to begin, the organist lowered the volume of his playing and the pastor emerged from beneath a white curtain. The church community quieted as he made his way to the pulpit, ruffling some papers in front of him and placing his hand delicately on the wood surface. His hand touching the lectern created a light thud that was amplified by the two microphones facing him, and called the few whispers that remained in the room to complete silence. That silence lasted for a few long seconds, finally interrupted by the pastor's bellowing voice. "Good morning, brothers and sisters. Isn't it a pleasure to be in the presence of the Lord this morning?" His words were followed by a smile so wide, it rivaled the glow from the stained glass windows and elicited smiles, cheers, and amens from the congregation.

A few latecomers, preoccupied with getting to their seats, seemed oblivious to the preacher's opening statement, as were others in the congregation whose full attention was not yet on the service. I was reminded of the response you'd get from students at the start of a classroom lesson after lunch or gym. The preacher repeated his greeting, this time with more vigor. "Isn't it a pleasure to be in the presence of the Lord this morning?" A smattering of amens followed. Apparently still not satisfied with the response, he repeated the question again, and then again, slowly increasing his volume and zeal until the entire church responded wildly with cheers and amens. The energy in the room, once everyone was in unison, was electrifying. As electrifying as in hip-hop when a high level of agreement is reached and people affirm it by simply saying "Chuuuuuch!"

During the service, the pastor spoke to hundreds of people, but the exchange seemed deeply personal. There were announcements and stories that invoked different responses from people seated in different parts of the church, but all were in communion. This exchange continued for a little over three hours with a few beautiful interruptions by the choir, who swayed back and forth as they filled the room with their voices, moving congregants across the room to stand and sing in unison, their arms raised; on occasion someone shouted out an affirmation. When the preacher delivered his sermon, the congregation remained fully engaged. With his words he alternately raised and lowered the levels of emotion in the room, bringing the congregation to its feet and then quieting them, seamlessly inviting them to read from scripture and then offering an analysis of the text.

The sermon was a mix of current events, biblical references, politics, and social commentary. It had a title, which the preacher announced before he began his sermon, and even an outline that he shared with the congregation. However, the sermon was free flowing and pulled from many different topics while making its point.

The scene described here is emblematic of hundreds of visits I made to Pentecostal black churches across urban America in preparation for writing this book. These spaces share rules of engagement and general norms and traditions that serve as powerful models for white folks who teach in the hood and can be used to transform the classroom.

Teaching the "Model Teacher"

I initially embarked on these church visits while working with a white teacher who had been recruited by the Teach for America program after graduating college five year before. This teacher, in his midtwenties, had been chosen by the school administration to become a lead teacher, and I was charged with spending the year preparing him for his new job. As I usually do when asked to work with a teacher, I began by observing the teacher in his middle school classroom in New York City, taking notes on his teaching style, asking students about their experiences in the classroom, and watching video of the teacher teaching. Based on my research into the teacher's practice, I would write a prescription for how he might improve his effectiveness in the classroom.

As is typically the case with young teachers who decide to stay in urban schools after fulfilling the two-year requirement of their recruiting program, this young man was thrust into a leadership role prematurely, but he welcomed the opportunity to take on more responsibilities. After meeting with him for the first time and watching him teach, it became clear that the school administration had asked him to become a lead teacher for reasons that had very little to do with the quality of his teaching. He struggled to connect with students, had difficulty getting them to respond to his questions, and didn't seem too concerned that he wasn't fully engaging students.

Prior to walking into this teacher's classroom, I had been sent a number of lesson plans he had written. As I studied them, I marveled at his attention to detail, and how calculated he was about identifying the tasks he wanted his students to complete and when he wanted them to complete them. Based on his lesson plans, I could determine what he was going to say at any given time during the lesson. He was so well prepared, he knew what he was going to be teaching at least three weeks in advance. However, the more I read what the principal had described as "model" lesson plans, the more concerned I was about how he planned to connect with his students. The lessons were so structured and inflexible that they restricted student involvement to a set time period for questions, and even these were planned for—the lessons featuring answers to students' "expected questions." Despite my misgivings, I decided to withhold judgment until I had a chance to visit the teacher's classroom; once I did, however, my concerns only grew.

There was such exactness in his delivery that there was no way for his students to take the lesson off-script. While the lesson looked great on paper, and may have worked well in another context, it didn't work for the urban youth of color he was teaching. More specifically, when following his lesson plan as he taught, I could predict how students would react and respond to different parts of the lesson. There were points where I could see that the hyper focus on writing tasks without context would get students frustrated, where it was obvious that the language was too complex to make the point and would confuse or bore students. I could perfectly time when eyes would roll and heads would begin leaning downward toward the desks. Unfortunately, the teacher was oblivious to these cues and made no adjustments to his teaching. Despite this lackluster performance in the classroom, he was consistently praised by school administrators as being a teacher with great promise who was expected to become a model for his peers.

I felt the administrators were misguided in their choice of a prospective model teacher, and began considering other candidates. I thought that maybe if I found the right person, the school administration would reconsider their choice. I went through the entire teaching staff in my head, and while many had the potential to be a lead teacher, no one had been teaching in the building for long enough to be able to take that role. But then I discovered that a gentleman who was introduced to me as the school's "dean of behavior" was also a teacher at the school. He was tall, black, and had an imposing voice that students responded to. I had never observed him teach, but it was obvious that students gravitated toward him, even though he often raised his voice and was in charge of enforcing the school discipline code. He had been at the school since it opened five years before and was at the time transitioning out of the classroom and into school administration, thus he only taught one class a week. One afternoon, I walked into this class and witnessed magic. The students were at the edge of their seats, waiting for him to give them instructions for their next task. The room was filled with music, the blinds were off the windows, allowing light to shine through the classroom, students were asking questions, some hovering by the teacher's desk to access materials. All were obviously fully engaged. The energy in the room was similar to being in a black church. The first word that came to mind as I saw the collective agreement and energy in the room was *chuuuuch!*

After leaving this class, I wondered why the ability to plan a lesson, and not the ability to connect with students, was the prerequisite for being a model teacher. In this case, being a model teacher meant being able to develop lesson plans that could be followed by any teacher across the country, reflecting the language of the newest academic standards. It had nothing much to do with students' learning. A teacher who would melt under the radiant heat generated by the questions of an inquisitive urban student, or would put students to sleep through a boring lesson, would have opportunities to spread their brand of teaching to other teachers despite its possible negative effects on students, and the fact that effective and powerful alternatives exist.

Teachers who believe they are gifted at their craft because they are seen as special by the school administration for reasons that have nothing to do with engaging students must be introduced to pedagogy as it is expressed among the neoindigenous. They must be confronted with the harsh fact that they are ineffective in the classroom. The teacher who was being groomed to lead instruction based on the quality of his lesson plans had no idea what it meant to engage and connect to students. He needed much more than a quick coaching session by an "expert" to help him become a leader. He needed to see what true engagement looked like.

When I spoke to him about the importance of engaging his students, he consistently asked that I work with the students on their ability to pay attention. When I raised the possibility that his lessons were ineffective with the students he was teaching, he stated that he had modeled his lessons "against the best ones out there" and knew they matched the curriculum and standards perfectly.

Over the few weeks that we worked together, we both grew increasingly frustrated. When I suggested that he visit the classroom of the dean of behavior, he was reluctant, and when he eventually agreed to observe that class, he was overly focused on what he perceived as poor classroom management, oblivious to the students' high level of engagement. The dynamic in the classroom was the opposite of what he perceived as an ideal learning environment, even though this one engaged students and his ideal did not. In short he did not understand his students' neoindigeneity, and the only thing I could think of to help us bridge the very obvious divide between us was a visit to church.

The reason that this teacher led me to church (besides driving me to pray that he either retired early or learned how to teach) was that this was the only place where he would get some insight into the realities of his students. Most importantly, it was a place where he could see a wider range of emotions from urban people of color than anything he had seen before. He did not know what true engagement looked or sounded like, had no clue about how to inspire urban youth of color, and had preconceptions of what teaching and learning should look like that did not match the needs of his students. In fact, the church visit that I had made just a few weeks before our initial meeting encapsulated everything that was missing from his teaching. Every moment in the church that morning would have been a pedagogical goldmine for this teacher. I hoped that a visit to a black church would show him how to create context, elicit responses from students, engage them, help them to make connections, and keep them attentive.

The beauty of the process I had witnessed in Harlem could be narrowed down to the preacher's awareness of the delicate balance between structure and improvisation. There were certain norms that both the pastor and the congregation followed, yet there was ample space for, and an expectation of, dynamic departures from the script. The preacher's ability to have control over the service while allowing the congregants to guide his preaching can be replicated in the classroom through an approach to teaching that I call Pentecostal pedagogy.

Lessons from the Black Church

Pentecostal pedagogy gleans teaching practices from the black church and is a necessary model for teachers charged with engaging urban youth of color in classrooms but who have no training in what it means to be neoindigenous and alienated from traditional school culture. An intervention like Pentecostal pedagogy brings the urban educator to church, or brings the church to the urban educator. It requires being a student of the ways pastor and congregants conduct a highly charged exchange, and not necessarily of the faith or religious practice of the church members. It also requires the educator to study the contexts of the gathering and the effects of the contexts on those that gather in that space.

Initially, I naively hoped that just by witnessing the pastor's style, the teacher I was working with would become a better teacher. Although he enjoyed the service, he struggled to learn from it because he was uncomfortable being the only white face in the congregation. He also decided that coming back the next week would not be possible because it would take too much time away from his lesson planning.

After a lengthy discussion about how the discomfort he felt that morning was analogous to the ways his students felt when they were forced to conform their neoindigenous selves to the "ideal student" he designed his lessons for, I decided that I would bring the church to the teacher. I collected videos of Pentecostal preachers and watched them with him, identifying the pedagogical moments in the sermons; I also collected video clips of different aspects of church services that modeled the best ways to create the right context for teaching and learning. These videos became the core of our professional-development sessions and led to a major shift in the way that he engaged with students, and also the way that I approach the work of preparing teachers to master their craft. The videos from black churches reminded me that teaching requires showing the learner (whether teacher or student) models of what is to be learned. In this case, it required having the teacher imagine who (if anyone) he was seeing when he created his lessons, and then showing him examples of how those lessons would differ if he was designing the lessons for the church congregation—which would require learning from the preacher.

I have found that the two most powerful elements of a Pentecostal service, as related to pedagogy, are the call-and-response exchanges between preacher and congregation, which results in focus and engagement, and the solemn call to the altar that moves them to be reflective. I share video clips of these parts of a Pentecostal service with teachers to demonstrate the power of effective teaching. Pentecostal pedagogy is an approach to teaching that reminds us that teaching is not just telling students what you know; it is about knowing *how* to share what you know so that it can be optimally received.

Watching video of these two elements of a Pentecostal sermon left the teacher I was working with in amazement. He couldn't fathom how the preacher was able to move the crowd so skillfully from excited and focused to solemn and reflective minutes later. We then undertook a closer study of the subtleties in each of the two videos, paying special attention to the preacher's voice inflections, the role of music in setting a certain tone, the flexibility that the church attendees had to sit where they wanted, the types of responses the preacher generated at different parts of the service, and the way the preacher led the service without commandeering it.

The ability to guide without controlling, to create the best context, to be flexible, and to make the crowd move is found in both the black church and in hip-hop. Rappers, who are often described as the teachers of the hip-hop generation, are referred to as MCs when they have demonstrated that they have the ability to teach. To MC or move the crowd is to be able to share information, spark thinking, invoke dialogue, and keep an audience engaged. Whether we are talking about preachers or MCs, both use music to create a context for engaging their audience and then utilize the context that has been created as a tool for sharing information. They both use call-and-response (e.g., asking the congregation the question "Can I get an amen?" and waiting for the audience to put their hands up and respond) to ensure the crowd is engaged, use the volume of their voice to elicit certain types of responses, actively work the room, and make references to contemporary issues or respond to cues in the immediate environment to enliven their planned/scripted sermons and performances. I argue that the use of these techniques, which fall under the umbrella of Pentecostal pedagogy, is necessary for teaching urban youth of color. Pentecostal pedagogy can be transferred into nonreligious or secular places by invoking the emotional responses that exist within the spaces that the neoindigenous inhabit together. If rappers can adopt the pedagogical approaches developed in the black church and use them to connect to audiences of young people, then teachers can and should do the same.

In addition to the church videos, I shared a number of rap performance videos, identifying the moments of heightened audience response that would invoke a chuuuuch moment with the teacher. The performers in these videos always had someone on stage with them to serve as an intermediary between the audience and the performer. The rap videos had a lot in common with the church clips. The teacher began to identify the nuances we had discussed previously. For example, he noticed that when MCs used call-and-response to draw the audience in, they employed a different tone of voice to get different types of responses to the same call-and-response phrase. On one occasion, he said, "Look at how he tells them to put their hands up, and then the way he asks them to throw up a peace sign for Tupac and Biggie. It's like he's asking when it's more emotional. Like it's a shifting of the emotions. There are times in class to tell the kids to do something, and then times to ask them. I can have them react differently. This is powerful stuff."

As we studied more videos and the teacher became more proficient in identifying the pedagogical processes that were rooted in the neoindigenous community, he began to see their value. Aspects of teaching and learning that previously had been dismissed as irrelevant to delivering a lesson began to emerge as significant. Slowly, he began to notice things like how comfortable and respectful attendees at the church were with responding to the preacher or affirming something he said. He noticed the prevalence of freedom and risk taking when church attendees decided to keep singing or emoting after everyone else had stopped. He realized that despite the free-flowing structure of church services and rap concerts, there were routines and protocol in place that ensured a cohesive exchange of information and ideas. This protocol is not written anywhere, not memorized to be spat out later on a multiple-choice test of knowledge or skills. It just is. In particular, the idea of "catching the spirit," when a member of the church community temporarily takes control of the moment from the preacher, was a key piece of many of our conversations. Through a study of these moments, we were able to identify that the teaching and learning experience had multiple leaders, not just the person who was nominally "in charge." If a student needed to take the class to a different emotional place or a different topic of conversation, the teacher needed to be like the preacher and not only allow it to happen, but celebrate it. This led to powerful conversations about the need for students to engage emotionally in order to learn from someone or something. Pentecostal pedagogy, and the hip-hop pedagogy that comes from it, is successful because it provides a safe space to identify, discuss, and express emotion. For the neoindigenous, this is a necessary prerequisite for being comfortable enough to learn within certain places. It is therefore a pedagogical skill to be able to both evoke and contain emotion in a way that supports free exchange among students, and between the students and the teacher. A Pentecostal pedagogue engages in the classroom with an elevated consciousness about neoindigineity.

Pentecostal pedagogy requires a different view of teaching itself. Here, teaching is a process where a context is created in which information is exchanged among people with the end result being an increase in the knowledge/information of everyone who takes part. This type of teaching is very different from the type that a traditional teacher does in an urban public school. It requires an understanding of, and appreciation for, the unique cultural dimensions of neoindigeneity. It considers those aspects of their experience that connect urban youth to their indigenous counterparts and utilizes them to create the appropriate classroom space. It considers the language of the students, and incorporates it into the teaching by welcoming slang, colloquialisms, and "nonacademic" expressions, and then uses them to introduce new topics, knowledge, and conversations. It acknowledges and provides an escape from everyday oppression (which may come from interactions with the criminal justice system or schools) by creating a space to vent these frustrations and escape them even temporarily in a powerful learning space, and it considers the ties the student has to the outside world (neighborhood/community), reaching beyond the classroom (place) to a shared community experience.

Of Barbers and Beauty Shops

On a beautiful fall afternoon at the end of October, a group of scholars sat around a magnificently decorated table in a grand room in the Faculty House at one of the most esteemed universities in the world. Their eyes, ears, and spirits were open and eager to hear from the guest of the day—a prolific rapper from Queens, New York, who proclaimed proudly early in his career that he was a "school dropout [who] never liked that shit from day one." Around the table, there were two college professors, three gentlemen who worked in the music industry, the rapper, and a group of brilliant Harvard undergraduate students.

As we all sat at the table, we mentally prepared for an amazing intellectual discussion. Unfortunately, no one seemed able to spark the conversation. In a room filled with degrees and awards, high grade-point averages, and magazine covers, there was no teacher in the room to set the context for learning. With no teacher to guide us, we sat in awkward silence looking up at each other every few seconds and exchanging head nods and empty smiles.

Before long, we were interrupted by an announcement inviting us to help ourselves to some food set out at a buffet table across the room. Relief filled every face as we used this moment to break the silence and make small talk about the weather and what was being served. However, before long, our empty chatter was once again replaced by the quiet murmur of an old heating system, awkward whispers among groups of two or three, and the occasional sound of silverware on plates. The impasse persisted until from somewhere in that room, among the many brilliant people assembled, a teacher finally emerged.

The teacher happened to be the most unassuming person in the room. He sat at the side of the table that was farthest away from the rapper. As it turns out, he was the rapper's barber and had traveled to the event with him. He observed us curiously as we struggled to start the conversation, and calmly enjoyed his meal as we spoke quietly among ourselves. Then he pushed his plate aside and joked about how good the food was as indicated by his empty plate. Everyone laughed. Having broken the ice, he then posed a question to the entire room. In a strong voice that pierced the silence, he asked, "What music are you listening to?" Answers came quickly from all around the room. Some mentioned specific artists, others mentioned genres, and eventually the rapper spoke about the current artists he was listening to. The people around the table commented on the performers he mentioned, and before long a conversation was taking place.

By asking the question, the teacher (not by profession, but embodying what it means to be a teacher) opened up the space for dialogue that gave everyone an entry point into the discussion. He started with a joke that made everyone comfortable, and then asked a question that everyone could answer. When one person named an artist who no one else knew, that person shared song titles and encouraged the group to check them out. Someone else mentioned a favorite song and two or three others excitedly affirmed it. A discussion started about what certain artists represented to the hip-hop community. As the level of engagement grew, Marcus (the barber) facilitated conversations about philosophy and sociology, history and music. He opened up a space for our guest to share much about his art, and the significance of his being invited to the university that day. A few times, Marcus would model for us how to engage the rapper, asking him a question and then slightly nodding to us encouragingly. That day, the teacher was not the brilliant rapper or the accomplished professors, it was Marcus, who was there that day because he was a great barber, but ended up showing us how to be a good teacher. After that meeting, I kept in contact with Marcus, and later had an opportunity to further discover his giftedness.

Every academic year, I teach a class on urban and multicultural education that focuses on innovative ways to connect to neoindigenous populations. The students who enroll in the class are aspiring and in-service teachers who are taking the class in pursuit of an advanced degree in education, and/or interested in teaching or conducting research in urban education. In previous semesters, I had invited a number of well-known professors/educators to deliver guest lectures. One semester, during the final five minutes of class, I announced,

"Marcus Harvey will be our guest lecturer next week." Students immediately reached for their iPads, laptops, and cell phones, excited to look up this name on the Internet. Over the course of the week, I got a number of emails from students who asked me to repeat the name of the prospective visiting professor. Many others sent notes informing me that they were unable to find any information on an expert in teaching named Marcus Harvey. I responded by assuring them that they did not have to worry about doing any research in preparation for the lecture, but should just come prepared to listen and ready to ask questions.

The next week, in a packed class with students and their guests filling every seat, I described the need for reimagining teaching, and then introduced Marcus Harvey and two other barbers who accompanied him. Marcus stood up and walked to the center of the room, introduced his two fellow barbers, and began to hold court. He started by mentioning that he was not exactly sure why he was invited to address them, or how qualified he was to deliver a lecture in front of a room of educators, but that he was happy to talk to them about his barbershop and clients. The students looked around at each other with confused smiles on their faces, but gave their full attention to the lecturer.

Marcus spoke about what a client expects when they go to a barber, and what he believes his moral responsibility to his craft requires when they sit in his chair. He said, "Clients walk into my shop to get a haircut, but as a master of my craft, my responsibility is to ensure that the client leaves the barbershop having had a personal experience with me that makes them want to come back. It's bigger than just a haircut." As Marcus described the difference between giving a haircut and creating a context where a person has a personal experience, the connections between what he was saying and previous discussions the class had had about teaching content versus connecting to students began to emerge. I would excitedly interrupt him at times to make these connections explicit to the students. I would tell students to play a scenario Marcus described out in their heads but replace the word *barber* with *teacher,* and *client* with *student.* Before long, students were making the connections on their own, and I watched from the back of the classroom in awe as my graduate school students got a very similar experience to the one I had been a part of a few months before.

As Marcus spoke, students began to ask questions about what they should do when a client/student comes in with a bad attitude, how to keep their sanity when the pressure of the work gets to be too much, and perhaps most importantly, what happens when your client/student comes from an ethnic background that is different from your own. Marcus talked about diffusing a client's negativity or anxiety through humor and story, addressing the larger circle around the client to create an inclusive space for people to voice their frustrations and concerns and release tensions, having other employees interact with the client, and most importantly, understanding that "cutting a white dude's hair is different than cutting a black dude's hair. I had to take time out to learn how to cut white hair. I needed to get new tools to give haircuts to people who weren't black because the texture of their hair was different. I really had to go practice a new approach."

After the lecture, the entire class seemed to have made the connection between what Marcus does in his barbershop and teaching. Perhaps the most important lesson they learned was that urban education requires a different approach from that taken in traditional classrooms. Teaching in the hood requires a very different skill set that those coming into the hood must first recognize they lack, and then train to develop. The strategies that Marcus employs with his clients issue from Pentecostal pedagogy. Infusing humor and story into the instruction, allowing the space for the release of tensions and frustrations, and welcoming the voices of the people you are sharing information with or providing a service to—these are tools used on the pulpit and in the barbershop, and should be used in the classroom as well. Marcus effortlessly created a space that allowed my graduate students to ask questions, but he also modeled how to engage an audience. He walked around the room confidently, validated each question before responding, and transformed the lecture into a conversation.

Educators who may not be comfortable visiting a place of worship can find in barbershops and beauty salons many of the same lessons from Pentecostal pedagogy. If the barbershop or salon that the teacher visits is within the neighborhood of the school or the community that the students are from, the teacher not only learns how to engage with students by observing the ways that barbers and hairdressers interact with their clients, but also has the opportunity to learn about the neighborhood, community events, and students' parents, siblings, and extended families.

By studying Pentecostal pedagogy and the ways it is expressed in places like barbershops and beauty salons, the educator learns how to value voice and foster family within the classroom. If one feels like what they have to say is of value in a particular place, they are more apt to transform the place into a community and partake in the activities that are valued within it. Within the urban classroom, valuing voice means providing students with an opportunity to have their thoughts, words, and ideas about the classroom and the world beyond it heard and incorporated into the approach to instruction. By accepting that student voice will be a major part of the structure of the classroom, the teacher must be prepared for a number of possible scenarios that may initially be uncomfortable for the teacher, will challenge both the structure of the traditional classroom and the teacher's authority, but will ultimately positively affect the teacher's instruction, and the students' learning.

Once the students' voice is valued, the educator can work toward fostering family—crucial for the neoindigenous. Within urban communities, particularly within socioeconomically deprived places, those who do not have traditional family structures often create their own with other members of their community. Consequently, the same social and emotional ties that exist within traditional families exist in neoindigenous communities among the wide range of people within these communities. This is seen in the "church family," "family gatherings" at barber shops and beauty salons, and many other complex variations of family that exist within these communities. These families may not share biological bonds but they do share values, language, and experiences (often around negative encounters with authority figures) that forge bonds as strong as or stronger than blood connections.

For the educator, knowledge of the process by which these familial bonds are created, and a command of the tools that support their creation, is integral to being effective. The best classroom teachers develop ways to make the classroom feel like a family that has its own distinct rules, ways of speaking, and power dynamics. Pentecostal pedagogy teaches us that once student voice is prominent in the classroom, and a classroom family structure has been established, issues that traditionally plague urban classrooms, like poor management and low participation, are quickly addressed or even self-corrected. Students with behavior management issues begin to self-manage and may even facilitate classroom discussions when there is a space for voice within the classroom family.

In the chapters that follow, I describe the chief complement to Pentecostal pedagogy in the form of tools associated with reality pedagogy. This approach consists of what I call the "Seven C's"— cogenerative dialogues, coteaching, cosmopolitanism, context, content, competition, and curation. I will use the frameworks developed earlier to make powerful points about the type of pedagogy needed to teach in the hood, and provide practical examples of ways white folks who teach in the hood can implement this pedagogy to improve their instruction.

CHAPTER 4

Cogenerative Dialogues

He walked into the classroom on the first day of school with an unmistakable air of authority, as if an invisible force surrounded him. His head high, shoulders straight, pants low, painted lines across his deep brown brow. On occasion, he would let his guard drop just long enough to flash a smile or a menacing scowl. He was intimidating, yet charismatic. That was his gift, and he brought it into the classroom.

She was the exact opposite. She was demure but deliberate about every step she took and keenly aware of everything that was going on around her. Her hand would rise as soon as the teacher asked a question, her homework was turned in as soon as it was requested, and she often volunteered to take the attendance to the office or make photocopies for the teacher. However, she found a way to disappear for group assignments or classroom presentations. When her peers teased her for being "too good" or "too quiet," she shrank into herself, visibly upset. It took her time to recover—and when she did, she was cautious about revealing it to others. She brought this sensitivity into the classroom.

In the same classroom with these two individuals was an overachieving female student who viewed her life in America as an opportunity to receive the education that her parents never had a chance to get in their home country. Her parents worked three jobs each and had no time to visit the school during open-house events or parent-teacher conferences, but one of them walked to the building with her every day. She described her father as a constant presence perched on her right shoulder, whispering stories about the sacrifices he had made to make it to America. He frequently reminded her about his now-deferred dreams of being a medical doctor. He told her how he'd excelled at science when he was in school and about the time in his village in Mexico when he singlehandedly delivered a baby with no medical equipment. Their tiny apartment smelled like the sandwiches he made for a living, and she carried that scent with her every time she left home and headed to school. She worked hard every day to ensure that she fulfilled her father's dream and became a doctor—a dream she could see actualized with every A she brought home on her report card.

I taught these three students a few years ago, and despite their ethnic and racial similarities, their shared age range and neighborhoods, each of them came to the urban classroom with unique stories and histories. As a teacher, I had to find an approach to teaching that would empower each of my students while addressing their collective needs. This proved to be virtually impossible given their very different personalities and those of the twenty-seven other complex beings I was responsible for teaching. At least this was the case until one afternoon in the school cafeteria when I witnessed an array of students of different ethnic and home backgrounds engaged in the process of teaching and learning on their own, without a teacher in sight.

Lessons from the Rap Cypher

One afternoon, after grinding through a lesson that was observed by the assistant principal, and then having a grueling post-observation meeting in her office, I decided to cut through the student cafeteria to get back to my classroom As I lightly jogged across the room, I spotted a group of students who had gathered together around a table. Emanating from this group of students was laughter, joy, and excitement unlike anything I had ever heard in the classroom. I walked toward them, temporarily forgetting I'd been headed to my classroom, in search of what it was that created all that positive energy. The six or so students were gathered around a lunchroom table rapping, clapping, and cheering for each other. They were in the middle of what is known as a rap cypher—a highly codified mode of communication and dialogue that the neoindigenous engage in on street corners and other places within urban neighborhoods.

One girl rapped while the others bobbed their heads in unison and "beatboxed"—creating sounds that mimicked drums with their mouths and hands. I had seen rap cyphers before, and even participated in them. However, I did not expect to see the three students I described in the beginning of this chapter actively engaged in the process together. These were students who seemed incapable of forging connections because of how different they were. However, because of their shared neoindigeneity, they found a platform for engaging with each other through the cypher. In this space, they were able to use the same mechanism (the cypher) to describe very different realities. They had organically created what the Brazilian educator and philosopher Paulo Freire described as a culture circle—where adults who were learning to read and write came together in an informal learning space and used their unique ways of speaking to become literate by sharing their understandings of the world and their place within it. The similarities between the hip-hop cypher and the culture circle speak to the universality of indigeneity and the ways that indigenous traditions have deep meaning for all marginalized groups.[1]

After seeing my students engage in the beautiful space they had co-created within the school outside the confines of the classroom, I began to think about how powerful the cypher could be for learning. I began visiting these students' cyphers in the cafeteria more often, which led to my attending cyphers on street corners and during community events and studying them as a pedagogical practice. I began traveling around the country to watch cyphers after rap concerts and witnessing them unfold on social media. In each instance, I would see people from diverse backgrounds, with different levels of skill and different personality types, create a space that allowed each participant to fully engage in, and gain something from, the fellowship with peers.

As I studied the cyphers more, I began to conduct experiments that were intended to test the potential of the cypher to engage neoindigenous populations across settings. In one experiment, I traveled to major urban cities across the United States with two rappers. In city after city, they were asked to stand on a street corner and rap to each other. In each instance, within minutes people from the area would join the rappers; some would begin rapping as well, and others would just stop and listen. In a few instances, and oftentimes without the individuals conferring with one another, the group would swell to some twenty people standing equidistant from each other in a circle, engaging in a complex set of activities that they already knew the rules of engagement for. Oftentimes, I would walk into the cypher and pretend not to know these rules, and study the ways that the participants in the activity taught me the rules of engagement by simply doing/modeling. Each time, I was included into the circle with care, and slowly introduced to the rules of engagement. In its basic format, one person at a time is at the helm of the cypher, while the other participants nod, cheer, and give each other affirmations in the form of oohs and ahhs when something profound is said.

The cypher transcends place and creates spaces where the neoindigenous provide clues to the outside world about to how to engage across differences and create an appropriate context for learning. The more I studied cyphers, the more I realized how they could benefit teachers who are looking for ways to effectively engage with students. More importantly, it became clear that the structure of the cypher could be merged with the culture of schools to create truly emancipatory new practices in classrooms.

One of these emancipatory practices (which merges the culture circle and the cypher) is the cogenerative dialogue, or cogen. In research projects aimed at improving urban classrooms, the implementation of cogens that draw from the structure of the hip-hop cypher and the spirit of the culture circle have proven to increase student interest, participation, and performance. Cogens are simple conversations between the teacher and their students with a goal of co-creating/generating plans of action for improving the classroom.[2] My work with cogens has shown that they allow teachers to more effectively deliver complex subject matter to students from different cultures, because they allow teachers and students to bridge their cultural divides *before* addressing content. In instances where the youth and the teacher are from different cultural backgrounds, as is the case with most urban teachers and their students, effectively introducing and implementing the cogen in a way that replicates the structure of the cypher has proven to be effective in motivating neoindigenous students to engage in dialogues with teachers in ways that allow them to share with their teacher their suggestions for improving the classroom.

Cogens in the Classroom: The Educational Cypher

In implementing cogens, teachers should introduce them in a way that does not make students see them as another school responsibility or assignment. They should also be presented in a way that allows youth to see how prominent the structure and goals of the cypher are within the dialogue. With youth, I use the words *cogen* and *cypher* interchangeably, wanting them to see them as synonymous. While the cypher within neoindigenous communities usually involves rapping or dance, I frame the cogen to students as a cypher that involves or pertains to education and the classroom.

Neoindigenous youth who have seen or experienced the cypher know the rules of engagement, which easily extend to the cogen. For example, the notion that only one MC (rapper) has the mic at a time easily aligns to the cogen requirement that only one person speaks at a time.

By introducing the cogen as a type of cypher, the teacher calls forth the students' neoindigeneity. The presentation of the activity as an extension of what youth do already validates their culture and positions them as experts even before the dialogue gets started.

Rooted in the structure of the cypher, cogens validate neoindigenous traditions within the academic setting. For white folks who teach in the hood, this means that they can be open about their ignorance of youth culture while welcoming it in the context of the cogen.

Cogens, in their purest form, are structured dialogues about the inner workings of the social field participants coinhabit. A social field is any location where human beings interact under particular rules and hierarchies established by society. It is understood that any person who spends time within a certain place is an agent of that place whose actions are somewhat predetermined by the structures in place. To have a cogen about a particular social field requires the belief that everyone who will participate brings tremendous value to the dialogue, because each has a unique perspective and vantage point. Those who participate in the educational cogen are viewed as experts on their own unique relationship to the social field that is the classroom.

The structures in place in traditional urban classrooms do not lend themselves to giving students a voice or a space in which to be valued and respected for their experiences. Students who populate urban schools are generally beholden to a "pedagogy of poverty" that rewards them for being docile and punishes them for being overly vocal or expressive. In response, and because they genuinely want to be successful in schools, many learn to repress their voices in order to not make any trouble. Young women of color in particular are not only encouraged to be docile but are academically rewarded for being "well-behaved young ladies" and reprimanded for asking too many questions or speaking out in class. Rewarding submissiveness occurs with boys as well, but its prevalence with girls leads to what I call "pretty brown girl syndrome." In a school system that positions black and brown boys as loud, abrasive, and unteachable, and that rewards black and brown girls for being submissive, teachers often give students good grades for being "nice and quiet" at the expense of ensuring that they are learning.

Cogens are a response to this brand of pedagogy because they welcome self-expression and value the voice of the student and student critiques of the classroom and school. When teachers engage in dialogues with students that privilege their unique voices, the students feel validated for who they are rather than who the teacher expects or desires them to be.

In research projects across schools in cities like New York and Philadelphia, researchers who have implemented cogens with their students find that teachers emerge from the dialogues with a deeper understanding of their students and the various strengths they bring to the classroom. Furthermore, teachers who act on the feedback they get from students have reported improvement in classroom participation and student performance in even the most challenging academic areas.

Structuring the Educational Cypher

While I have established that the most successful cogens look and feel like hip-hop cyphers, it is important to note the specific structures that distinguish the educational cypher. These dialogues begin with a small group of four students who meet with the teacher weekly. The meetings are held "in secret," and not shared with the rest of the class.

Teachers who are looking to engage in reality pedagogy in order to better connect with students should begin the cogen process by fully understanding that its primary goal is to elicit information from the students about the learning environment and gain direct feedback from them on all aspects of the teacher's instruction. That information is then used to improve the classroom environment. There must be some preparation on the part of the teacher for the potentially negative feedback the students will provide.

Below I outline steps for the successful implementation of the educational cypher.

Identify students as possible participants in the cogen based on the different social, ethnic, or academic groups of which they are a part (e.g., a first cogen could consist of a high-achieving and low-achieving student paired with an engaged and disengaged student). The most significant aspect of the cogen structure is ensuring that different demographics in the classroom are represented. By demographics I refer to the specific backgrounds of students; understanding how they may classify each other based on academic ability, skills, or talents; and identifying the social groups/cliques that are formed both inside and outside of the classroom. For example, a teacher may be able to identify students as Latino, but should also be able to identify students as being of Dominican, Puerto Rican, or Mexican descent. This type of information about who is in the classroom helps the teacher to create cogen groups that accurately reflect the diversity of the students. To begin the selection process, the teacher must actively elicit information from students. A teacher may choose to have students fill out cards in the beginning of the school year asking them to respond to questions that would not come up during the course of a traditional class. Questions like What is your favorite subject? What is your favorite meal? What is your ethnicity? Who is your favorite artist? Where are your parents from? give insight into youth realities that the teacher can use to create cogen groups.

For cogen sessions, particularly the first one, it is imperative that the teacher ensures that the initial group of students is not homogeneous. While students may have similarities in certain areas, it is their differences as revealed in the cogen that lead to rich dialogues. Research indicates that the selection of a wide range of students in the initial dialogue leads to more productive and long-lasting sessions in the future. Such diversity in the cogen also leads to more opportunities for the teacher to understand the different realities of students in the classroom. For example, a student who is successful on classroom exams experiences the learning environment differently from one who doesn't know what that type of success feels like. Similarly, an English-language learner and a native English speaker will have very different experiences of the same classroom.

To assist in the process of identifying the "opposites" necessary for cogens, teachers might dedicate a notebook to their observations of the unique demographics in the classroom, as a path to understanding the various connections among students. I suggest that teachers create lists of categories from their first day in the classroom and continue to build these lists as the school year develops. The development of these lists should occur with a goal of uncovering as many variations as possible among students, which in turn allows the teacher to understand and appreciate the dynamic nature of the classroom. Furthermore, engaging in this process allows the teacher to tailor instruction to the individual students in the classroom rather than teaching to a generic "urban student."

Invite students who are identified as possible participants to take part in the dialogues. The purpose of the selection of students who are opposites, or who represent the diversity of the classroom, is to allow for different voices to be heard. However, students will be reluctant to come to the dialogues if they misperceive the intention of the teacher, or feel like they are being singled out (this is particularly the case with students who struggle academically or are from groups viewed as "less than" in the classroom). Therefore, it is important for the teacher to be very deliberate about not only who is invited, but also how they are invited. The invitation process should be respectful of students, their time, and their status/reputation in the classroom.

Teachers must remember that the invitation is exactly that, an invitation; students should not be pressured to participate and should feel free to opt out. Participation in the cogen should be seen as entirely voluntary; the cogen is not a traditional class assignment on which they will be graded. The teacher should also tailor the invitation to the individual students being invited. To show respect for students' schedules, the invitation should include the expected length of time for the dialogue. It should also allow for students' input in terms of when the dialogues will take place. Teachers should be mindful of putting students at ease and emphasizing that participation in the cogen is a privilege, not a punishment. For example, the initial invitation from the teacher can be posed in a similar way to the following: "I would like to have a conversation with you and a few of your classmates for two to three minutes after class. No, you're not in trouble [before the student even responds]; I just wanted to get your thoughts on a few things."

This type of nonconfrontational invitation, coupled with the use of humor in letting the student know immediately that they are not in trouble, eases tensions. Furthermore, requesting the student's thoughts during the invitation and prior to the cogen positions the student as a person of value from the onset and affects their willingness to participate. The use of humor at this early phase is supported by research in education that shows that humor in the classroom creates less threatening social scenarios and makes students more comfortable communicating with the teacher. The need to make the student feel comfortable is particularly necessary because the teacher is introducing the student to a type of practice that is outside of the school norm. Teachers should expect a certain amount of skepticism and reluctance from students invited to participate in cogens. A student's first reaction to such an invitation may likely be apprehension, prompting questions like Did I do something wrong? Am I in trouble for something? What are we going to be talking about? Why are we doing this? Who else will be there? Do I have to come?

The best way for the teacher to respond to questions like these, and others that arise, is to acknowledge the questions and offer very general, conciliatory answers. In fact, my experience tells me that supplying students with too much detail increases the likelihood that they will opt out of the cogen. It's best to allow them to draw their own conclusions/answers about what the cogen is about. If a student asks if they are obligated to be a part of the cogen, the teacher could respond with a question like, "Do you think I would force you to come to a meeting?" A response like this tends to spark the student's curiosity, and gives them a feeling of control. To further ease students' concerns, the teacher could explain in general terms their intentions for the cypher: "It's a conversation that is definitely not the same old thing going on in school. I picked the best group of students I could find to help me out on this project." The point is to ensure students that the dialogue is not intended to simply replicate or expand on the negative experiences they may be having in school.

The following is a sample exchange between a teacher and a student invited to participate in the cogen.

> STUDENT: All right, I'll come to the cypher thing, but I don't know if I will have the time for it after school because I have stuff to do.

> TEACHER: We will meet for a few minutes during lunch or a few minutes after school. It will be you and about three other students, and I'll be there too. Would you prefer during lunch or after school? Whichever works best for you.

> STUDENT: What if I want after school and everybody else wants lunch. Then what?

> TEACHER: We'll keep working till we get a time that everyone agrees with. The decision is really up to you.

Empowering the student to decide when the dialogue will take place (during lunch or after school) sets the stage for the cogen. In fact, I would argue that the above exchange was a test by the student to see whether or not the cogen was truly a space where her voice and needs mattered. Once students recognize that they are valued, they welcome the opportunity to engage in the dialogue.

Arrange the physical space for the cypher and establish the rules. Once the invitation has been extended to the selected students and a time has been set for the first cogen, the next step is for the teacher to focus on structuring these dialogues in ways that reflect the physical structure of the cyphers that the neoindigenous already engage in. This means that the seats in the meeting place are positioned equidistant from each other and in a circle so participants can make eye contact with each other much in the same way that rappers arrange themselves in the hip-hop cypher. Ideally, during the cogen, there is music playing in the backdrop (like in a rap cypher) that provides a rhythm to the conversation and creates a classroom ambiance that promotes dialogue. Choose a space that ensures the cogen group will not be seen or overheard by other students or adults, an empty class-room or office space, for example.

Teachers should plan the cogen around a meal or a snack. This immediately sets the tone of the dialogue as one of sharing and fel-lowship. Teachers should make every effort to have food available for the students once they arrive, and create a space where students are comfortable breaking bread together. The teacher can either compensate the students for their time by supplying a snack, or have them bring their lunch to the cogen (if the meeting takes place at lunchtime), but sufficient time should be allowed for eating together. This alleviates tension and supports student connectedness.

During the initial dialogue, the students go over the "rules" that will guide their cogens. Ideally this should happen as participants eat their lunch or a snack, in order to create an informal structure for the conversation. It is important for the teacher to let students know that these rules are simply guidelines to ensure that the cogen is successful and that all voices are heard; they are not punitive. Students should be assured that the rules apply as well to the teacher to ensure that he or she runs the dialogue appropriately.

The first of these rules is that during the dialogue, no voice is priv-ileged over another. This rule can be extended to include the group's acceptance that all students have equal turns at talk and have ample opportunities to constructively challenge each other and the teacher. The second rule, which comes from neoindigenous practices during performances (and is most evident during the cypher), is that there is only "one mic." This means that only one person has the floor at any given time. Others may support or affirm, but only one person at a time serves as speaker. The last rule, which is the most significant one, is that the dialogue leads to a cogenerated/agreed upon plan of action that everyone who is a part of the dialogue must work toward when they return to the classroom.

Individual handouts or a small poster clearly stating the rules should be provided to participants. The rules should be given to students in the most succinct version possible:

- No voice is privileged over another, or, "Everybody eats, everybody speaks."
- One person speaks at a time; or "one mic."
- The cogen results in a plan of action for improving the classroom.

In most scenarios, students will ask the teacher to elaborate on the rules that are presented or will ask questions about what could happen if the rules are broken. For many students, this line of questioning is an attempt to test the teacher's willingness to adhere to the rules because the rules seem to favor the students. When these questions are posed, it is the teacher's responsibility to let the students know that the rules prevail even if it means that the teacher talks less and students get to speak more. The teacher must impress upon the students that if the established "rules of engagement" are violated by any member of the group (for example if one person dominates the dialogue or is not respectful of another member), the cogen group is collectively responsible for addressing the issue. This is the case even if the person who violates the rules is the teacher. To address the violation of the rules of engagement in a respectful manner and to ensure that no person feels outnumbered or alienated by the group, all dialogues within the cogen adhere strictly to the neoindigenous "one mic" philosophy of hip-hop/rap cyphers. For example, when rappers perform to and for each other in cyphers, they engage with a general understanding that no voice is privileged. Participants have equal opportunities to rap, and one person at a time holds the mic (whether an actual microphone or an imaginary one). Phrases like "one mic," used in everyday neoindigenous interactions, establish for the students that the cogen is not an extension of the traditional classroom but a dynamic learning space that reimagines what happens in schools. This structure works particularly well with small groups, and prepares the teacher for having similarly powerful conversations with an entire class.

Sparking the Initial Dialogue

The teacher must focus on taking advantage of this dynamic learning space from the get-go. Sparking a dialogue that allows students to see the power and privilege of participating in the cogen involves framing and naming the initial members of the group as special advisers of a "secret board" that in essence controls the class. The students are made aware that they are part of this board and that they will be influencing classroom management, and they are encouraged to come up with a special name or "tag" for themselves. The goal at this point is to ensure that the initial cogen fosters students' excitement about participating in the process. In one instance, four students who had been selected as cogen participants walked into a classroom and were immediately handed certificates by the school principal that identified them as "advisory panel to the teacher." The principal shook their hands, thanked them for being part of the group, took pictures with them, and then exited the room as the teacher invited them to sit down and have a snack so they could begin their first cogen. The students had not yet even understood what they were in the room for, but knew immediately that they were special.

The second goal of the initial dialogue is for students to experience positive results from being a part of the conversation. While the dialogues will eventually be led by students, the teacher needs to take the lead initially in modeling cogen participation. Therefore, the teacher should present an issue that the group can solve together. The first cogenerated action should be one that focuses on a small issue and an obvious and easily answered one. Some examples of dialogue topics that are suitable for the first dialogue and that lend themselves to the initial engagement of all students are

- suggestions of something the teacher can do within the first or last five minutes of the next class to either open or close the lesson;

- identification of a good/positive practice that the teacher enacts in the classroom that he/she can do more often; and
- identification of a practice all students in the cogen group can collectively do (including the teacher) to engage the students in the next class.

These types of topics are likely to support the engagement of all students in the cogen group and can lead to plans of action generated by the group that the teacher can easily implement during the students' next class. For example, if the students decide that the teacher should thank students who arrive early to class rather than shame them when someone comes in late, and the teacher models this behavior, students who are part of the cogen group quickly begin to recognize that they have a voice that has an impact on what happens in the classroom. This makes them more likely to participate in future dialogues and also connects them to the classroom and the teacher in new ways. This process prepares students for future dialogues where the nature of the issues they address will be more complex, and where they will have to critique not just the teacher, but the school, society, and themselves.

After the initial cogen, and when the participants in the dialogue return to the classroom with their peers, it is not only important for the teacher to be deliberate in enacting the cogenerated idea or suggestion, but to be explicit in letting participants know that he or she is doing so. This does not require any sort of official announcement, but the enactment of subtle indicators to students who were part of the cogen group that the plan of action is being implemented. This is particularly challenging for white folks who teach in the hood who are unaware of the nonverbal modes of communication of youth. My suggestion is for the teacher to ask students about nonverbal cues that they can use in the classroom to signal that they are implementing a suggestion generated in the cogen. Students have suggested that the teacher give eye contact and a head nod or lightly place their hand on students' desks to indicate the enactment of the cogen plan. Enacting these nonverbal cues allows students to recognize the moments when the teacher is attempting to connect to them, and valuing their voices as participants in the cogen. When the teacher enacts a specific action that the cogen members can associate with a plan generated by the group, an awareness of the need to follow through on the plan is created.

Continuing the Cypher

After the initial cycle of moving from cogenerated plan to classroom practice, the next step is to repeat the process until it becomes ritualized. This cannot happen unless the cogens meet regularly and establish their own routine. I argue that every consistent patterned action over time becomes a ritual and that practices become rituals once they have been set in place and have been successfully repeated at least three times. Therefore, it is important to enact this cycle (cogenerated plan agreed upon by group, classroom implementation of cogenerated plan) at least three times with the same initially selected students so that they begin to see the entire process as more than a passing fad and more of a ritual that is part of being a student in a classroom that values their thoughts and opinions.

For all students, consistency is key to effective teaching. For the neoindigenous (like the indigenous), consistent shared rituals are at the essence of the culture and important for setting the tone for learning. In an essay about rituals in baseball, the sociologist George Gmelch discusses the ways that rituals give those who follow them control and confidence to maximize their potential within the spaces they occupy.[3] When students in cogens meet regularly and ritualize the process of cogenerating and then implementing certain plans of action, they become empowered in the classroom and comfortable with talking to each other about their own learning. When students feel comfortable in cogens, the rituals they developed often take on aspects of neoindigenous culture that the teacher may not be a part of. The more privy the teacher is to these cultural expressions (in the form of cogen rituals), the more likely it is for the teacher to connect to students and even build new rituals with them.

Once connections are made with the students in the group and rituals are shared, one person from the cogen group is asked by the teacher to invite another student from the class to participate in the next cogen. This means that there will now be five students rather than four in the cogen group with the teacher. This group includes the four original members and "the newbie" who is introduced to the entire process by the four original members. However, before we get to the point where there can be other students in the class joining and benefiting from the cogen, the following steps have to be taken:

- The initial cogen group should meet at least three times so that the cogen is established as a ritual and so that students see the plans of action they cogenerated being implemented in the classroom.
- During the third cogen with the original group of students, the teacher should ask one of the cogen participants to invite a friend from the class (outside of the initial group) to participate in the next cogen.
- The fourth cogen should include members of the initial group (the original four students) and the newly invited student. The new student is introduced by the other students to the cogen process, and is reminded of the improvements in the classroom that have recently happened as a result of the previous cogens. The "secret" of how the teacher has improved or why the classroom is running better is revealed to the new student.
- After this fourth cogen with five students, the student who invited the new member to the dialogue is asked to opt out of the next round of cogens and concurrently asked to take on an assigned role in the classroom (like video recorder). The teacher explains that this will help keep the cogen group small, and emphasizes the significance of the new role the student will be taking on. (See chapter 6 for further details on

the roles a student can take on after opting out of the cogen group.) The next cogen will consist of student experts who are now in their fifth cogen and the new student invited by the former cogen group member. These students begin a new cycle of generating plans of action that will be implemented in the class.

- This new configuration of students then meets three times, and then the process is repeated: another student from the initial group is asked to invite a peer to the next cogen. The student experts introduce the new student to the group and explain the group rules. The student who invited the new student is asked to opt out of the dialogues and take on a role in the class.

Two of the steps above require a bit more clarification. The first is the process whereby a student invites a peer to the group and then opts out of future cogens. The second is the process whereby students from the initial cogen describe the cogen process to the newly in-vited student. In regards to the first process, teachers often ask why I suggest that they not be the ones to invite students after having identified the initial group. My response is simple. It can be awkward and uncomfortable for both teacher and students when teachers ask students to talk outside classroom time. The teacher's participation is initially necessary in getting the cogens going. After that, how-ever, the students should be the ones taking on the responsibility for keeping the dialogues running. This empowers students, positions the teacher as just another participant in the dialogues rather than the leader, and removes the association of the cogen with a teacher/school-owned activity.

With regards to the opting out of a student, the process has to be done carefully so that the student who is asked to leave does not feel as though his or her voice is no longer valued within the group. The best way to avoid this is to once again solicit student voices in the opt-out process. The conversation might play out something like this:

TEACHER: We have had these cyphers for a while now, and I think we can do more to get other people involved. I need other students to be a part of this, don't you agree?

STUDENTS: Yes (almost in unison).

TEACHER: I also need someone from this group to work more in the classroom on collecting and distributing assignments for the class so I can concentrate more on implementing the suggestions you guys come up with in the cogens.

(At this stage, most if not all of the students raise their hands or volunteer to take on the newly introduced role in the classroom, because they see it as continuing on with the agenda of the cogens, which is to improve the classroom.)

TEACHER: Well, I don't want everyone to take on this responsibility in the classroom because it is a lot. In fact, the person who takes on this role will not be able to be a part of the cogen group while they have this role because it is so important. The thing is that this person can invite someone else in the class to be a part of the cogen. They then become an honorary member. Almost like they graduated.

STUDENT A: I'll volunteer. I can handle that.

STUDENT B: I don't mind doing it either.

TEACHER: It's your group and your class. I'll let you guys decide and let us know what you decide later.

By ensuring that the students make the decision to opt out of the dialogue and take on a new role in the class, the teacher positions them as key players in the classroom. In addition, the teacher positions opting out as a thing to aspire to.

The rotation of members after three sessions has many benefits, most significantly the way that it impacts the group dynamics within the classroom. When the new student becomes connected to the cogen group, the student is oftentimes engaging with a group of students whom he or she may have never interacted with before. For example, a student who is performing well academically is oftentimes part of a social network that consists of other similarly engaged students. However, that student is engaging in a cogen with students who might not be as engaged in the classroom. This dynamic creation of networks changes the way students interact with each other when they return to the classroom and challenges the cliques that typically form in the classroom based on student similarities. Most importantly, it calls forth powerful indigenous traditions related to fostering family and connections that are at the essence of improving teaching and learning.

While the process discussed above is a pedagogical practice that all teachers could benefit from, it is especially important within neoindigenous classrooms, where the cultural differences between teachers and their students may otherwise go unaddressed.

CHAPTER 5

Coteaching

Early in my college teaching career, a few months after I obtained my doctoral degree, I walked into a graduate-school class I was assigned to teach in a predominantly white Ivy League college a few minutes early, took a seat at the front, opened up my laptop, and caught up on some work as I waited patiently for my class to arrive. Before long, two students walked into the classroom. I barely looked up as they found their seats, gave each other slight head nods, and placed notebooks and laptops on their respective tables. Because there was still about fifteen minutes before class, I figured I would use that time to fill out the seemingly endless number of forms I had to complete as a new faculty member. As it happened, I was so engrossed in filling out the forms that I barely noticed the room filling up with students. They walked in as strangers and sat quietly at their seats without speaking to me or to each other. I kept at my task with the full intention of stopping a minute or two before class and introducing myself as their professor. However, when I finally finished my paperwork it was a minute or two after the start of class and a quiet murmur had begun to develop among the assembled students.

Before long, it was silent again. I decided I would use this opportunity to conduct a little experiment. I turned to a young white student sitting behind me and quietly said, "Can you believe this guy is late on the first day?" His response was simple and expected. "I know.

Ten-minute rule and I'm out of here." He must've responded loudly enough for the person sitting next to him to hear, and before long, just about everyone in the class was looking toward the clock and commenting on the late professor. The silence had been broken and, having been given a reason to complain to each other, the students formed a quick bond. Conversations ensued as they connected to each other based on the fact that their instructor was late, and I even responded with smiles to some of the comments. Just as it seemed they might be getting a bit too restless, I stood up and introduced myself as the professor.

The room once again fell silent, and students seemed surprised, uncomfortable, and even a bit embarrassed. Acting like nothing had happened, I proceeded to hand out the syllabus, discussed the assignments that would be due, and then began the lecture. The air in the classroom was tense. Students who had jovially complained about the teacher being late and who had smiled at me as the class cracked jokes with one another now sat stone-faced. The more I ignored what had happened, the clearer it became that I had created a divide in the classroom that wouldn't go away on its own. By veiling my identity, I had been able to form an easy connection with everyone in the classroom. When I finally announced that I was the professor, I locked myself out of the social network the students had developed. My exclusion made it challenging to connect to them. I had become an outsider to the group, and over the course of the semester, I began to question my effectiveness as an instructor. My confidence shattered, and I slowly tried to rebuild it. Unfortunately, I did this by growing critical of my students and the ways they engaged with each other.

As the semester progressed, the impasse created by an innocuous experiment intended to test the social climate of the institution caused the white middle-class identities of my students to slowly become an issue for me as an instructor. Admittedly, I probably came to the class with a bit of a chip on my shoulder as a black man who had mostly attended urban public institutions not knowing what to expect in a predominantly white Ivy League space. I began to notice the ways that the students spoke to each other, the terms and expressions they used, and the general familiarity that they had with each other that I was not privy to. I became painfully aware of both my blackness and urbanness, and in many ways grew hypersensitive to the expressions of white middle-class norms like the slower paced, nonoverlapping speech of the students. The point here is that when differences between the teacher and students are present and go unaddressed, they multiply quickly. For me, these differences seemed stronger than the connection I had made with students on the first day of the class when bantering with them about the tardy teacher.

In order to effectively teach, I realized that I had to find a way around the tensions that existed in the classroom. Since students spent such an inordinate amount of time talking to each other right before, and oftentimes during and after, my class, I decided to use their social ties as a teaching strategy rather than attempt to fight my way into the networks they had created. My next set of assignments encouraged them to take the helm, teaching within the networks they had created. I found some of the resulting conversations too slow-paced, very different than the way I would have approached teaching, a reflection of their privileged standpoints, but they learned from the experience and clearly loved it. End-of-year evaluations mentioned how the class had "started off on the wrong foot, but really got much better toward the middle and end of the semester." One student commented, "I really enjoyed learning from my fellow master's and doctoral students. They were so insightful." Allowing the students to teach their own class became the solution for me, and is as great a strategy for black professors who teach white students in the Ivy League as it is for white folks who teach in the hood.

The tensions I felt when it became clear that I was not culturally aligned with my students can be felt by any educator who does not share the same cultural background as their students. The key to becoming an effective educator is acknowledging the differences between students and teacher and adjusting one's teaching accordingly, which often requires nontraditional approaches to teaching and learning.

Rethinking Classroom Instruction

In a powerful article on culture and education, the psychologist Michael Cole described two research studies that highlighted the work of scholars who pushed the boundaries of traditional teaching.[1] One was based on teaching of indigenous populations, and the other focused on the neoindigenous. The first study was based on the work of Kathryn Au and described the ways that an "altered curriculum structure" rooted in the ways that native Hawaiian children engage/communicate with each other increased these students' reading scores. This work highlighted the indigenous modes of communication of Hawaiian youth that included rhythmic conversations and overlapping speech and suggested that the use of these modes of communication in the classroom supports the learning of the students.

The second study focused on the work of Carol Lee and described the ways that the everyday practices and experiences of African American students (who I describe as neoindigenous) could be used to leverage a more complex understanding of standard literacy. In other words, using the culture of the youth, which teachers often view as antiacademic, ends up helping these youth in the classroom. In each of these studies, the key theme that emerged was the potential of youth language and experience to positively impact teaching. These studies confirm that employing indigenous and neoindigenous youth knowledge is the key to teaching neoindigenous people. I argue that additionally, the optimal way for youth language and experience to be used as a teaching tool involves having the youth themselves do the teaching. For this to happen, students have to be seen as teachers. By this I mean that students in traditional K–12 schools have to be viewed as partners with the adults who are officially charged with the delivery of content and be seen/named/treated as fellow teachers or coteachers.

The practice of coteaching has a storied history in education and is currently commonplace in just about all urban schools. In the most popular form of coteaching, two adult teachers work in tandem to teach the class. If certain students don't understand the instructor, or if one teacher is having an issue delivering the content, a coteacher will spring into action to support their peer. Ideally, coteaching has all the teachers involved in the process of designing lessons and teaching and often involves consensus among the teachers about who teaches what content based on their expertise. With this approach to coteaching, the two teachers are so deeply in sync with each other and are so committed to consistently responding to each other that they may spend more time studying each other's habits and dispositions than their students.

In another form of coteaching, a veteran and novice or student teacher both lead a classroom. The veteran has the responsibility of teaching the other how to teach, and the student teacher (usually from a local teacher-education program) is there to learn how to teach from the expert. In this iteration of coteaching, the veteran models how to teach and then allows the novice to take the helm of the classroom at different points of the semester to "practice" under the supervision of the veteran. In this scenario, the novice is observing the master teacher and learning to teach by implementing what has been observed. This process of learning to teach from the practitioner expert is usually supported by classes that the novice teacher is taking at a university or training program. Many of these programs support the notion of a master teacher that can teach aspiring teachers by modeling instruction. The entire process is one that affirms a belief that expertise in teaching comes from the person who has spent the most time in the role of teacher. Implicitly, it also sends the message that the closer one mimics an established model of teaching, the better one is at the craft of teaching. The model described above runs counter to my belief that expertise in teaching is much more complex than time spent teaching. If a teacher has spent an entire career enacting practices that do not meet the needs of the neoindigenous, then time spent enacting these practices only serves to make the teachers experts at maintaining oppression through their teaching. If these experts are given the role of mentoring new teachers, the cycle of dysfunctional teaching for white folks who teach in the hood continues.

A final model of coteaching that I will describe here is prominent in special education and inclusion classrooms and is a hybrid of the two versions described above. In this model, classroom teachers licensed to work in general education classes are partnered with special education teachers either in special education classrooms, where the goal is to ensure that students get content despite being diagnosed as having special needs, or in an inclusion classroom (mixed with both special education and "regular" education students). The goal in these classrooms is often to rehabilitate youth with behavior problems and/or acclimate special education students to mainstream classrooms with students who are not special education students. In these classrooms, one teacher is often charged with the delivery of content while the other is responsible for behavior and other issues related to the needs of the special education students. Here, there are two types of experts in the classroom: the teacher of content and the person who is more in touch with the students and their socioemotional needs. The students are well aware which teacher occupies which role and because of hierarchies that privilege the content expert over the other teacher, inherit a respect for one teacher and a disrespect for the other.

In each of the scenarios described above, the potential of coteaching to significantly affect the learning of the neoindigenous is never truly actualized because the responsibility to teach is never placed in the hand of those best equipped. In fact, coteaching, despite its potential as a transformative academic tool, has done little to close achievement gaps or make neoindigenous youth feel like part of the teaching and learning process. I argue that this is the case because increasing the number of teachers in the classroom without increasing these teachers' knowledge about the students and where they come from does not amount to much change. This is evident when we consider the fact that neoindigenous youth overpopulate special education classes that are mostly taught by two teachers, and that the chances of leaving special education after being placed in that system is slim for all students, and consequently, close to impossible for the neoindigenous.[2]

In response to the broken version of coteaching in special education classrooms in particular and in classrooms generally, I propose a reality pedagogy–based version of coteaching. This version deconstructs the ways that we previously have viewed coteaching by identifying and focusing on the transformative power of having more than one classroom leader/teacher in the classroom, and then extending the role of teacher/leader to students. This may require positioning the traditional teacher as a student in the classroom. Coteaching within reality pedagogy involves the transfer of student/teacher roles so that everyone within the classroom can gain the opportunity to experience teaching and learning from the other's perspective. Furthermore, it requires a redistribution of power in the classroom that returns to the essence of teaching—privileging the voice of the student.

The Coteaching Classroom: Student as Expert

One of the chief goals of coteaching in reality pedagogy is to train the teacher to teach in a way that reflects the needs of the student by creating classroom spaces where teachers are being trained by their students. Coteaching in this model is predicated on the fact that the teacher cannot fully meet the needs of students unless the students have an opportunity to show the teacher what they need and then demonstrate what good teaching looks like for them. This requires the teacher to be transparent about aspects of their work that students do not usually know about. The teacher has to present the students with the larger contexts/information that shape how and why they teach the way they do so that the students can model how to work with the existing structures/resources and still be effective. I argue that the resilience required for being neoindigenous in contemporary America equips young people for being able to navigate the challenges of urban teaching.

I am reminded of one classroom in which I conducted research, where a teacher participating in a cogen group was sharing with students the challenges of teaching with a structured curriculum, little resources, and students who weren't always engaged. He was interrupted by two members of his cogen group who essentially told him to stop the "pity party." One student in particular interrupted his rant by saying, "Aren't the five of us sitting here? Who cares how they want you to teach? We can cover everything [content] they want. We have a team here. You're spending so much time complaining about what you can't do when we can just talk about what we can do. You know how many issues I have in my life? You don't see me complaining all day." In that moment, I was reminded of the resilience and grit that the neoindigenous naturally possess by simply existing within challenging socioeconomic environments. It also reminded me that when given an opportunity to teach with the same challenges that traditional teachers do, they will show how it can be done because they are well equipped to adapt to conditions that are less than ideal.

Coteaching in reality pedagogy provides neoindigenous youth this opportunity to model good teaching by drawing from the three models of coteaching described earlier to create the ideal conditions for a reality-pedagogy-based model. Drawing from the first type of coteaching I described, the reality-pedagogy version focuses on creating opportunities for collaboration among experts. However, instead of having two teachers work together to create a lesson, two students or more are asked to not only teach the class but take on all the responsibilities that the teacher has for delivering the content effectively. This includes writing a lesson plan, aligning it to standards, identifying examples to be used during the lesson, finding teaching resources, arranging the seats in the class, and finding a method for the assessment of the teaching.

Given the responsibilities the students now have (that the teachers previously had), the teacher has to provide them with the same resources that other teachers have when teaching. This means that the teacher has to provide the students who are coteaching with previous lesson plans, teacher manuals, websites the teacher gathers resources from, and any other teacher materials that are used to supplement instruction. Once these materials are shared with students, they are given the full responsibility of teaching and are then graded by the teacher on the quality of their lesson plans and criteria that the teacher is usually assessed on. Rather than grading students for tasks like homework assignments and tests, the reality-pedagogy coteaching model assesses their content knowledge through how they design and teach their lessons.

From the second and third type of coteaching described earlier, coteaching in reality pedagogy follows an apprenticeship model that allows a novice to learn from an expert about how to teach. The difference here is that the neoindigenous student is positioned as the expert (in delivering information to other neoindigenous students), and the teacher is positioned as the person who needs to learn about the ways to teach to the neoindigenous. This way of thinking is often challenged by traditional teachers because it means that their credentials and degrees are now given very little value when compared to the lived experiences of the students. I was challenged by one teacher in a New York City public school to consider the implications for saying that students can be just as good as teachers with degrees. He asked, "Are you saying that a master's degree in education is useless? Aren't you sayin' that the job is so easy that even a kid can do it?" My response was "That is exactly *not* what I am saying. I am saying that the job is so layered and complex that those who live it every day are probably better equipped for it than those who don't. An advanced degree in education is absolutely necessary for anyone who is going to teach. However, for white folks who teach in the hood, it must be supplemented with much more."

Coteaching in reality pedagogy requires that teachers acknowledge that they may be an expert in their content, or at teaching that content in another location/setting, but not at teaching it to the neoindigenous. The process also requires that teachers let their students know that they are not only students but teaching experts whose knowledge about how to teach has tremendous value. This value for the students must then be displayed in the classroom through deliberate practices where the teacher is indicating a role shift and signaling to students that he or she is taking on the role of student. For example, while students are teaching the class, it is important for the teacher to sit in a seat where a student normally does and not interrupt the teaching. While in the student's seat, the teacher may takes notes on the ways that the students teach, document what they are doing differently from what the teacher would do, and pay attention to the content that is being delivered. Particular attention should be paid to the examples that students use and the ways they interact with each other; it is in these small expressions of neoindigeneity through words, expressions, and examples that the magic of teaching is revealed.

The goal here is for the teacher to incorporate what is observed from students' teaching into their own instruction. For example, after teaching a lesson on Newton's laws of motion a few years ago, and struggling to get students to understand the real-life application of the concepts, I started describing what would happen if we had two marbles on an endless frictionless surface feet away from each other, and what would happen if one marble was pushed to hit the other. My thought was that students would find this imaginary scenario fascinating and that it would help them grasp the concepts I was trying to teach. However, after providing this example with all the enthusiasm I could muster, students looked up at me either completely confused or disinterested.

Later that day, with another class, I decided to see what would happen if I gave students the opportunity to teach the same lesson. I invited two students to coteach the lesson I had previously taught. I handed them the materials I used to design my lesson, gave them a quick tutorial on the concept, and assigned them to write a lesson plan instead of completing a traditional homework assignment. The next day, after reviewing their lesson plan, I was astounded by the depth and detail in the lesson they had designed. I then invited the students to teach their lesson later in the day. As they stood in front of their peers, I became so enamored with their teaching style that I began to note how they engaged with their peers. The new coteachers gave everyone equal attention, walked around the classroom freely, and most importantly, instead of giving an example about marbles on a frictionless surface like I did, they used an example of someone riding a New York City subway, and what forces acted on the person's body after someone pulled the emergency brake. Instead of the disinterest that came from my example the previous day, the student coteachers' example sparked a powerful conversation about unbalanced forces, Newton's laws of motion, and how they apply to everyday life.

As the students and the coteachers engaged in this powerful conversation, I jotted down the example about riding the subway that the students used and was sure to write even more detailed notes about how they chose to describe that example to the class. I then went home and closely studied my notes and their lesson plan. I practiced my delivery of their example in the mirror till I had perfected it and then walked into the school the next day armed with a confidence and expertise about teaching that came directly from my new coteachers. In front of a class who hadn't yet been introduced to Newton's laws, I followed the lesson plan developed by my coteachers. As I taught, I described the example of riding the train my coteachers used and almost immediately the students engaged in ways that they had not done when I had taught the lesson previously. At one point, there was a collective "ohhhhhhhhhhh" from everyone in the class that lets any teacher know that clarity has been reached. I nodded excitedly as the lesson began to resonate with these students, knowing full well that having students serve as coteachers provided me with an opportunity to teach in a way that was directly informed by what the students needed in order to be engaged. I could not have made that type of connection on my own.

As stated earlier, coteaching in reality pedagogy focuses on a willingness to share all the resources the teacher has with students who will be doing the coteaching. This includes all the information gathered over the course of the academic year about the class and about teaching the subject at hand even when the information garnered is developed with and by students. In other words, it is just as important to glean information from students on how to teach better as it is to share the successes of their teaching strategies with them and future coteachers. The more information about the kind of instruction that students respond to within a particular setting becomes available, the better the tools are that are developed, and the better equipped future coteachers are for enhancing their teaching and learning.

With the availability of new teaching tools, students approach researching, preparing for, and teaching a classroom lesson with a newfound motivation that surpasses anything that could be generated in the traditional classroom. As the student takes the helm of the classroom and uncovers new approaches to teaching, there is a positioning of both the traditional teacher and student as co-learners. Within this new classroom structure, both students and teacher learn the nuances of each other's culture and how to see the classroom from each other's perspective. The student learns responsibility, puts in the effort it takes to prepare a lesson, and develops empathy for the struggles of the teacher. At the same time, the teacher observes lessons taught by students, takes notes on the ways that the student enacts pedagogy, documents the specific examples the student uses, takes note of the way the student/coteacher interacts with peers, and learns how to teach in ways that reflect the realities of students' experiences.

For the neoindigenous, coteaching in reality pedagogy provides a counternarrative to the pedagogy of poverty that inscribes an anti-school identity on youth who are actually deeply engaged in school and committed to academic success. As students collect resources, prepare lessons, and share ideas, it again becomes apparent that they love the process of teaching and learning when they are a part of it. I have had experiences where students who have previously cotaught lessons stand up in the middle of a teacher's lesson visibly upset because "it" (the teacher's instruction) was "being done the wrong way." When coteaching is enacted, students develop the agency or power to act in ways that challenge the oppression they are often conditioned to be silent about. They are not only vocal about when teaching is not working for them; they model what the type of teaching they need looks like. They reveal their core identities or true selves; which for the neoindigenous involves being free from any structures that inhibit them from being fully actualized. In urban classrooms, to be fully actualized is to be free to teach and learn on their own terms.

Implementing Coteaching in the Classroom

Coteaching is a natural outgrowth of the educational cypher. Ideally, coteaching is implemented in the classroom after a cycle of cogen sessions has taken place with a group of students.

The steps outlined below fall into three categories. The first consists of the preparation stage. The second involves the introduction of coteaching in the classroom. And the final one ensures that coteaching is incorporated into regular classroom practice.

Introduce coteaching during a cogen session to students who have already gone through a three-cogen cycle. Coteaching begins with students from a cogen group who have gone through at least three cogen cycles and have seen their suggestions implemented in the classroom. Cogen participants are most amenable to putting themselves out on a limb for the sake of further improving classroom instruction.

Introduce the idea of coteaching to cogen students in a way that emphasizes their position as experts. You might say something like, "Now that we have figured out some things to do to make the class better, and we have implemented some of your suggestions for the class, I want a few of you to actually teach the class and show me how it's done." Usually, students will volunteer to teach and may ask if they can work as a group. This provides an opportunity for the teacher to build on the relationships that have been initiated in the cogen and allow youth to teach in duos or trios. This is particularly helpful when the teacher has selected a cogen group that represents the diversity of the classroom. By planning and delivering the lesson together, the group can move toward tighter cohesion across groups and model it for the rest of the class.

Select a volunteer or volunteers to be the coteacher(s) for an upcoming classroom lesson. Provide these students with the topic they will be coteaching and ask them to bring with them to the next cogen meeting the resources and teaching materials they will use to teach the lesson. The teacher should take a few moments to describe to students the types of resources he or she uses in formulating lesson plans. It is also important for the teacher to encourage students to bring in items of their own choosing as opposed to replications of what the teacher traditionally brings into the classroom. Rather, the students should be asked to bring in items that are reflective of the ways that teaching and learning occur within neoindigenous communities, or that the students think would work best for them and their fellow students. This is important because many youth have become acculturated into urban schooling in ways that silence their neoindigeneity, and adopt styles of teaching that they think the teacher will accept rather than an approach that engages peers who share their culture. When this happens and these youth are given an opportunity to teach, they spend more time emulating their teacher than introducing their way of teaching to the teacher. Therefore, it is important for the teacher to make the goals of coteaching clear: to foster family, to give voice to students, and to help the teacher learn from students the best ways to connect with them.

Utilize the next cogen meeting to coplan a lesson with the students who will be coteaching. Once students have shared their teaching materials with the cogen group, the teacher should work with them to plan the lesson. While the goal of coteaching is to have the students teach in innovative ways, it is important for the teacher to let students know that teaching is not done without preparation and that the process of designing a lesson (even if it is based on neoindigenous ways of knowing and being that they have expertise in) should be well thought out and mindful of the time allotment given to the class.

The coplanning session should begin with the teacher sharing the materials he or she uses to teach, such as the teacher's manual for the textbook, lesson plans from previous years, and Internet websites used for accessing data. Each of the students who will be coteaching should then be asked to introduce the materials they chose for the lesson.

Teachers should provide students with a general overview of the content that the students will be teaching in a mini-lesson of sorts for the cogen group. These students are given a preview of the lesson, are allowed to ask questions about the content, and then work toward developing a lesson on their own based on the content the teacher has taught, their independent preparation, and any ideas that they have developed in the course of sharing the resources they brought with them to the cogen group.

If the students are apprehensive about being in front of their peers, the cogen session can be used to allow them to rehearse their teaching and refine those parts of their lesson that they may not be completely comfortable with. This part of the preparation for teaching in the classroom should also include an introduction to the format of the traditional lesson. For example, students should be aware of, and in many cases instinctively follow, the traditional "workshop model" structure of the classroom, which includes having a larger goal for the lesson reflected as the "aim" or "objective" for the lesson, having a "do now" or "motivation" activity that serves as an entry point to the lesson to come, and hands-on examples and opportunities for students to reflect on the lesson at the end of the class period. However, prospective coteachers should be encouraged not to feel committed to this structure, but have room for innovation.

Assign coteachers a homework project in which they are asked to enhance the lesson that was begun in the cogen, and provide them the tools, feedback, and reinforcement to further develop the lesson. This simply means that students who have gone this far in the process of coteaching are given an opportunity to fine-tune the lesson they initially developed with the teacher in the cogen. This provides an additional opportunity for the students to take the lesson to a level where it becomes saturated with the students' neoindigeneity and also gives them an opportunity to see that the teacher is not looking for a lesson that replicates his or her own teaching but instead is informed by the students' individual gifts and viewpoints.

In engaging in the coteaching process, students should receive positive reinforcement from the teacher, and some of this reinforcement should be in the form of classroom currency. The currency of the classroom is grades just as the currency outside of the classroom is money. If we value practices like coteaching, we must compensate students who engage in the practice with extra credit and better grades. If students are rewarded with good grades only for performing well on written tests and following instructions, they get conditioned into thinking that tests and classroom behavior are the only things that schools value. In many ways, not compensating students for taking on special projects in the classroom can be more damaging than their receiving bad grades on required tests or for bad behavior. In fact, when students get bad grades for not engaging in school in the ways they are expected to, there is some satisfaction that comes with knowing where one stands within the institution. When they do engage in powerful ways like coteaching and still fail to be recognized and compensated academically, the sense of alienation from schooling can be tough to overcome.

Students who engage in coteaching should not only be given extra credit on exams and other classroom assignments, they should be celebrated for the extra effort they are taking in the classroom. In many of the successful examples of coteaching that I have either led or researched, students who were engaged in coteaching were given exemptions from certain class assignments, received extra points on classroom tests or exams, and even had the opportunity to contribute to the design of classroom tests and other activities.

This shows the student that there is value in being fully engaged in school and their education, and consequently encourages efforts to express their full selves in the classroom.

Immediately prior to the students' teaching the lesson, perform a quick review of the students' lesson plan to ensure that content is accurate. This step is purposeful, simple, and quick, and is intended to ensure that the content the students are teaching is correct. They may already have been graded for their lesson, encouraged for being willing to teach it, and supported by their peers in the design of the lesson. This is simply a final affirmation of the students' work. It provides the teacher with the opportunity to give the students a final vote of confidence that conveys to them that the teacher is comfortable having them take the helm of the classroom. This step should not take more than a few minutes, and if there is something that is inaccurate in the students' content, the teacher may mention it, but should *not* seek to correct it at this point. Rather, the teacher takes note of this piece of the lesson and prepares to address it from the perspective of a student while the lesson is being taught. For example, in one of the coteaching sessions I observed, a student who was teaching the class used the terms *distance* and *displacement* interchangeably as she taught. However, she gave such amazing examples about how to measure distance and the units for measuring different distances that stopping her lesson before she even started would have been counterproductive. Here's how the lesson proceeded:

STUDENT A (coteacher): So this car was going at like twenty miles per hour. Driving real slow too. The car was like a 600 Benz. No tints. Clean. Just stunting around the block. Driving around till he stops at the same spot. How long do you think he'll go in an hour and a half?

STUDENT B: Gotta be like thirty miles, twenty for the hour and then ten for the half of that.

STUDENT A: You sure? Think about what I'm saying.
(short pause)

STUDENT B: Yup. Definitely thirty miles.

STUDENT A: No, his real distance is zero if he ends up at the same place he started. You calculated right though, that's how far he traveled. Your math is right.

At this point, the teacher, who had been sitting in a seat among other students, raised her hand, waited to be called on, and engaged in the following exchange:

TEACHER: Thanks for calling on me. Just wanted to ask a quick question. If he ends up at the same place he started, is his *distance* zero or his displacement? The book I'm looking at says displacement. You want to clarify?

STUDENT A: Give me a sec . . . Ohhhhh, right. That was what I was trying to get at. You guys still with me? If you end up at the same place, you still have your distance, but your displacement is zero. Let me give you guys a few more examples. I need two volunteers to come up here.

The student continued to teach the lesson, and provided a number of examples that the teacher took notes on and used later in other lessons she taught. This process allowed the student to feel comfortable, did not interrupt the process of coteaching as it was being enacted by the student, and allowed the teacher to learn a number of practical examples that she could then incorporate into future lessons. Therefore, before coteaching is enacted in the classroom, the teacher has to be aware that there may be moments when he or she needs to interrupt or correct (whether because of content or even the students' unconventional ways of teaching). It is important for the teacher to prepare for ways to make his or her points without disrupting the student's lesson and to do so respectfully—without undermining the student in her position as teacher of the lesson.

After the lesson, provide direct feedback to the coteacher(s). After any class where students have served as coteachers, it is critical that all students have an opportunity to reflect on the experience. This is accomplished by having all the students engage in a reflection on the lesson that gives direct feedback to the coteachers. This can be either a traditional written reflection or a "share out" where students discuss the experience and give each other feedback on the lesson. This dialogue is important because feedback from peers is essential for both the student coteachers and the traditional teacher, not only for improving future coteaching sessions but also for the teacher to learn about the most effective aspects of the coteachers' instruction. This exchange is a powerful moment in the teaching and learning process because of its role in undoing traditional and oppressive teaching in a way that deprograms students from the type of teaching that keeps them silent, and that they are in many ways conditioned to.

To solicit written feedback/reflections, the teacher might provide students with writing prompts/guiding questions that invoke deep reflection. Such prompts might ask, for example, What part of the lesson struck you as most effective or memorable? What was said or done and how did it make you feel? If you were the person who was teaching, what is it about the lesson that you would do the same? What would you do differently and why? In what ways was this lesson similar to, or different from, previous lessons? These types of questions invoke a critical response to the coteaching experience and give the teacher an opportunity to gather powerful data on the type of teaching that works for their neoindigenous students. It also serves to continuously improve the coteaching experience going forward, and draws other students into the coteaching process.

Creating the Space for Peer-to-Peer Teaching

The fundamental principle of coteaching in reality pedagogy is that the neoindigenous student is the expert on the best way to deliver information to others who are a part of their culture; the more opportunities students have to both teach and learn from their classmates, the better off they are in regards to understanding content. When I discuss coteaching with educators, they often respond by saying that they frequently invite students to come to the front of the class to answer questions, which they see as the equivalent of coteaching. But reality pedagogy requires moving beyond a superficial rendering of traditional coteaching that happens to include students for only a few minutes. Coteaching in reality pedagogy not only focuses on having youth teach a class, but also includes creating a structure in the classroom where students are given ample opportunities to teach peers one-on-one and take the reins from the teacher if the instruction does not meet their needs in the moment. This may mean that a student interrupts the lesson while the teacher is teaching to offer an alternate way of solving a problem or describing a concept.

Teaching in this way involves adopting new rules of engagement in which there is shared power between students and teachers, and peer-to-peer communication is encouraged during the class. Exchanges in this new type of classroom must then reflect the structure of conversations among the neoindigenous. For example, the native Hawaiian speech patterns mentioned earlier and the rap cypher serve as models for how to exchange in classrooms where a reality-pedagogy version of peer-to-peer coteaching exists. This means that students in the classroom may at times talk over each other and their teacher and speak at higher volumes than would be traditionally accepted because the focus is on ensuring that students learn in a way that reflects their neoindigeneity rather than the norms of the traditional classroom which may not facilitate true learning and engagement for them. This type of coteaching may also mean that the students spend a significant amount of time talking to each other about the content and are encouraged to do so. This process leads students to be more comfortable in the classroom and creates opportunities for them to participate in the classroom in a way that makes it easier for them to authentically disclose their academic strengths and weaknesses. The inclusion of neoindigenous forms of communication, including having students take the helm, creates an entirely new classroom that moves from "place" to "space." The space becomes a communal one in which all are deeply invested in the emotional and academic well-being of the entire classroom community.

I conducted research on/with a group of thirty students in a classroom where cogens and coteaching was practiced, and then observed these students across other classrooms over the course of an academic year. In the classroom in which coteaching was practiced, the students were noticeably more open about their academic challenges and willing to work with their peers within the classroom. In this class, cogens and coteaching were occurring weekly with at least one lesson a week taught by students. The energy in the class was different. Students moved freely from seat to seat, speaking to each other about content. They spoke at a higher volume with more passion when they communicated with each other and their teacher, rarely ever asked to be excused from the classroom, and demonstrated an obvious level of comfort with each other and with the instructional content.

In this class, students were quick to point out aspects of the lesson that they did not understand and were then supported by peers who felt they could help. However, these same students were painfully silent about sharing their academic challenges in other classrooms. They spoke in those classes only when the teacher addressed them directly or asked a specific question related to the content being taught. In these classes, they spoke for shorter amounts of time and their participation seemed limited or somehow obstructed (fewer raised hands and fewer questions asked). In interviews about the classrooms where they did not engage much, students would often identify the race/ethnicity of the teacher as a challenge to their learning in addition to a bevy of other complaints about everything from the class rules to the way the seating was organized. During one particularly striking interview, one student mentioned that a teacher "talks mad white and boring like the guy from the Clear Eyes commercial," referring to a popular caricature of an older white science teacher played by Ben Stein on television. In the reality-pedagogy classroom, even with an older white male teacher, race was not seen as an impediment. Students commented, "He's a cool white dude" or, "I don't even be noticing he white sometimes." This is not to say that cogens and coteaching erased the whiteness of the teacher, but whiteness was not perceived as a challenge to the students' learning.

In this class, a student once stood up in the class without being called on, walked to the front of the classroom, grabbed the marker from the teacher, and began teaching when she thought he was being ineffective. When situations like this happen, the reality pedagogue knows that it is the responsibility of the teacher to simply move out of the way and allow the student to teach. In another classroom in this traditional urban school, walking up to the front of the class and interrupting the teacher in this way would be considered threatening, disruptive, or disrespectful. However, when coteaching is established in the classroom, students are encouraged to take ownership of their learning process.

The coteaching moment described above unfolded organically, and is commonplace in classrooms in which students are celebrated for having the courage to express their lack of understanding or their dissatisfaction with the way content is being taught, as well as for their willingness to support their peers. The teacher that allows/ encourages peer-to-peer teaching transforms the structure of the classroom. Once the context has been set for the neoindigenous to be their authentic selves, they make deep connections with their teachers, their fellow students, and the learning process.

CHAPTER 6

Cosmopolitanism

One of my most memorable experiences as an educator occurred in my third year of teaching. Finally feeling like I knew what I was doing in the classroom, I had begun to form the teaching philosophy that I would come to call reality pedagogy. Among the practices I was instituting was inviting students to come in before school a couple of days a week, just to talk. Most mornings, only a few students showed up unless there was a cogen scheduled. When they did come in, they typically spent the time listening to music or talking to each other about sports, television shows, or neighborhood gossip.

During one of these conversations held on a Monday morning, a student informed me that she wouldn't be able to attend class the following Friday. It was a rare occurrence for students to tell me about an absence so far in advance, and so I thanked her for letting me know. She then began to talk excitedly to her friends about why she was going to be absent. She was traveling to Disney World with her father. She told us that this was going to be her first trip on an airplane, and that she had not seen her father in over a decade. The conversation about the trip continued until the school bell rang to start the day.

The next morning, the first thing this student did when she walked into the class was to remind me that she would not be in class that Friday. Again I thanked her for the notice, and she responded with an excited smile.

On Friday morning when I walked into my class, I spotted the student who was supposed to be on her way to Disney World sitting in the classroom with her notebook open, fully prepared for the classroom lesson. I was taken aback when I saw her but tried to conceal my surprise. My mind raced as I began to think about why this student was in school instead of off on a visit with her dad. Did her father change his mind about the trip? Had some other situation come up? Concerned, I observed the student closely throughout the day until we had a chance to talk, growing increasingly angry as I wondered how her father could cancel on her after not seeing her for ten years. I then imagined all of the hurt and disappointment she was feeling as she sat in class. She, however, seemed to be just fine. She completed her assignments, interacted with her friends, and handed out classroom materials just as she normally did. Throughout the day, she was as pleasant as she usually was, and this caused me to grow even more concerned.

I was convinced that she was masking her feelings and deflecting her emotions. As the day came to a close and she walked back into my classroom to get her coat and books, I took the opportunity to ask her if she was okay. She seemed confused by my question and said, "I'm great. We had a great class today." I asked her if she wanted to talk, and again she seemed confused, so I finally asked her directly about the trip. "What happened with your father?" I asked. "Are you okay? Do you need anything?" As my questions came pouring out, she touched my arm and said, "Oh, is that what you were asking about? I'm fine. I had to cancel on him yesterday." I was stunned by this response, but before I could ask another question, she said, "When I knew he was coming to see me I was excited, but I forgot that the trip was on a Friday"—Friday is our classroom lab activity day. "I am the class lab equipment distributor," she went on to say. "If I didn't come to school, who was going to give out the lab equipment? I had to cancel."

Without further explanation, she smiled, grabbed her things, and left to join a group of friends who were waiting for her at the door. I was completely floored by what she'd said, and it didn't quite make sense to me. However, as I walked out of the school and made my way home, the significance of what had happened became clear. This student had felt responsible for the learning of the other students in the classroom. Somehow, over the course of that academic year, we had created a family in that classroom that she was more loyal to than the father she hadn't seen in a decade. She felt responsible for the learning of her peers, and in many ways over the course of that year, her peers made it clear that they felt responsible for her learning as well.

When I got home from work that day, I called the student's mother to verify that everything was okay at home. She told me that her daughter had decided not to go on the trip to see her father that weekend because she had a job to do at school. She'd called her father and told him that she was willing to leave for the trip after school on Friday if he could change her flight. When it turned out that the flight couldn't be changed, she opted to go to school instead. While this way of thinking may defy logic for many people, it defines cosmopolitanism and the way it plays out within urban classrooms. A young person who is emotionally connected to the classroom as a cosmopolitan space will not only be willing to learn in that classroom but is committed to that classroom. In reality pedagogy, cosmopolitanism is an approach to teaching that focuses on fostering socioemotional connections in the classroom with the goal of building students' sense of responsibility to each other and to the learning environment.

As a philosophy, cosmopolitanism is often traced back to Greek tradition. Anthropologists like Gustavo Ribeiro describe it as a way of being in the world that focuses on an individual's embodiment of tolerance, sensitivity, and inclusiveness of others in the process of being a "citizen of the world." I argue that although global citizenship is a powerful construct, it is built by first developing a cosmopolitan ethos in local spaces like classrooms. I see the roots and manifestations of cosmopolitanism within indigenous and neoindigenous culture both historically and in the contemporary. The indigenous may not necessarily see themselves as citizens of the world, but they do see themselves as connected to, and extensions of, the universe. For the indigenous, these universal connections always begin with a reverence for the land they inhabit and the immediate spaces they occupy. Consequently, I adopt an indigenous brand of cosmopolitanism that focuses on students getting an opportunity to feel as though they are valued and respected, a full active citizen of the immediate classroom place and space they occupy. This means that they are involved with every aspect of the operation of the classroom, and are responsible for ensuring that citizenship in the classroom is both enacted and extended to everyone who occupies the same place and space. The teacher is the facilitator of this process in identifying roles that the students can fulfill and tasks they can perform that connect them to the classroom. The teacher's task is to let students know how important they are and how essential their jobs and roles are to the functioning of the classroom. This process involves making students aware of how each of them (through performing their tasks) becomes responsible for ensuring that the class runs well.

While cogens focus on developing plans of action for improving the classroom, and coteaching involves the expansion of the role of the student to include that of teacher, cosmopolitanism, as it is enacted in reality pedagogy, focuses on developing deep connections among students across differences such as race, ethnicity, gender, and academic ability as they work to ensure that they move collectively toward being socially, emotionally, and physically present and committed to the classroom they share.

In addition to creating new connections among students through the roles they adopt in the classroom, cosmopolitanism functions to heal divides (across ethnicity, gender, and perceived academic-ability lines) among the neoindigenous that may have been created in the world outside the classroom, but that affect how students connect to each other within it. By taking responsibility for their distinctive roles and serving each other in the classroom, they are given the opportunity to reenvision their relationships to each other and to the world outside school.

Roles and Responsibilities in the Classroom Family

To develop and foster a cosmopolitan ethos in the classroom, one of the first things a teacher must do (ideally at the beginning of the academic year or a new semester) is to identify the possible roles that everyone who comes into the classroom can take on to help it function properly. This includes roles tied to classroom learning, as well as those related to the social, emotional, and physical functioning of the classroom. By this I mean that student roles should include anything and everything needed for the classroom to function well. Desks have to be arranged, the floors have to be swept, teaching materials have to be organized, and the technology has to function properly. In a cosmopolitan classroom, these "nonacademic" responsibilities are just as important as those involving learning content. The "things that need to be done" are then taken on by students in their roles as equipment distributor, blackboard eraser, technology supervisor, desk arranger, assignment collector, guest greeter, seat arranger, floor sweeper, music coordinator, and even joke teller. Tasks undertaken by school staff such as custodial workers, school secretaries, and school administrators might be shared with students in a supplemental role. For example, if the custodial staff normally sweeps the floors after school, a student or group of students in the classroom could assist as the "after-class cleanup crew." The process of assigning roles should allow for volunteers. Depending on the tasks required, a teacher may choose to assign more than one student to a role. For example, three students may be assigned to clean up the class after a science lab while only one would be responsible for collecting assignments.

During this process, students should be introduced to what cosmopolitanism means in the classroom. A working definition I have used in explaining the cosmopolitan classroom is that it is a space where each student is a full citizen, responsible for how well the class meets the collective academic, social, and emotional goals. Students

are to be assured that the roles they take on in the effective functioning of the classroom are just as significant as, if not more important
than, doing well on classroom tests. They are graded on and receive
academic credit for their performance in these roles. If a student does
not do the task associated with a role, it is not going to be completed
by anyone else, and it will not only affect that student's grades, but
the ability of the rest of the class to learn in the optimal environment. In one case, a student was assigned the role of "eraser of the
chalkboard." While it may be perceived as an insignificant role, it
was clear to students that it was an important role when the student
assigned to it skipped class one day. That day, there were notes that
I wanted to write and that students needed to copy. However, because the eraser of the chalkboard did not come to school that day,
the board did not get erased. While other students volunteered to
complete the task, I ensured that no one did. The fallout from the
student's failure to perform his assigned role results in healthy peer
pressure from the class in holding him accountable for the disruption.

This approach runs counter to everything that teachers and students know about traditional teaching and its reliance on grades and
individual achievement as the only things that matter for youth to be
successful in school. However, with grades and positive affirmations
being provided to students for connecting to each other and exhib-
iting a cosmopolitan ethos, they soon begin to realize that this new
model of teaching and learning aligns closely to neoindigeneity and
their desire to support each other and their community.

Cosmopolitanism and the Neoindigenous

For white folks who teach in the hood, and any teacher who feels
unsettled by the misalignments between the culture of youth and
their own ways of knowing and being, the way forward is to view
tension in the classroom as an asset for creating a truly cosmopolitan
space. Sociologist Ann Swidler argues that it is in these unsettling
moments that people can co-create practices and philosophies that
establish a powerful new culture. I argue that it is in the acceptance

of their vulnerability in these moments that teachers begin to move from place to the emotion-laden spaces that the students inhabit. In other words, the teachers' acceptance of their vulnerability connects them to students who are often vulnerable because of how they are positioned in society. It is this joint vulnerability that is the prerequisite for change.

The typical response that a teacher (or anyone for that matter) has to feeling scared or vulnerable is to try to exert power over students (or anyone perceived as "other"). This is why teachers of urban youth of color become strict disciplinarians, and why students often alienate peers whom they view as different. To counter this phenomenon, humans have to be reconnected to each other through new and shared cosmopolitan practices.

This crafting of new and shared practices in the classroom social world requires an understanding of the racial, socioeconomic, dominant language groupings that exist in the classroom. Furthermore, it requires an understanding of the privileges that certain individuals have because of the groups of which they are a part. The point is not to force everyone to be a part of the dominant culture, but rather to move everyone to be themselves together. The current education system rewards both students and teachers who blindly assimilate into an anticosmopolitan and anti-neoindigenous school structure. The celebration of a homogenous student identity and denigration of expressions of neoindigeneity force many among the neoindigenous to assimilate into a set of school norms, which requires them to repress their authentic selves. For example, in a middle school classroom I worked in, a student was repeatedly celebrated for "sitting quietly on your own" while another was consistently scolded for "speaking too loudly with your friends." In one instance, the student who was praised smiled and sat at his desk with his hands clasped together while the one who was scolded responded to the teacher by saying, "But I was just trying to help them solve the math problem. They needed help so I was trying to help them." The teacher ignored the student's defense of his action, and then began to praise the student who sat quietly alone.

In many ways, teachers are hardwired to look favorably upon students who remind them of themselves. Scientists have identified mirror neurons that fire in us when others act in ways that we find familiar. In other words, the teacher wants to see herself in her students even if that runs counter to who her students are. Unfortunately, over time, the student described above, punished by his teacher for being "disruptive" when he was simply trying to help his peers, learned that being docile and passive was a favorable behavior in the classroom. He learned to repress his instincts to learn together with his peers in a way that reflected their neoindigeneity. The teacher had created an anticosmopolitan classroom, and students learned the modes of behavior needed to be successful in this place. Students became conditioned to engaging in the classroom in a certain way, consistent with the teacher's expectations.

The noncosmopolitan classroom results in alienating the neoindigenous. Their brilliance is denied because it doesn't fit into the existing mold and is consequently labeled antiacademic. This type of classroom forces students to deny their natural abilities and talents, and punishes those who refuse to comply while concurrently placing at a disadvantage those who seek to acclimate. These students become conditioned to spend their entire lives working toward assimilation into the white middle class. Unfortunately for them, assimilation comes at a cost to their neoindigeneity and, ultimately, their self-worth.

Philosopher Kelly Oliver recounts in a *New York Times* article the story of three Latina employees of a white-owned insurance company in "a heavily Hispanic neighborhood" in Amarillo, Texas.[1] The women were hired because they spoke Spanish; their employers hoped to drum up business from the Latino community. Their presence did bring in a lot of Latino customers. However, later in the year, two of the employees (Ester and Rosa) were fired for speaking Spanish at work. Their white employers, who didn't speak any Spanish, did not appreciate their employees speaking Spanish when customers weren't around. They felt uncomfortable or threatened by their employees' language and culture and asked the three Latina employees to sign a pledge that included an agreement to speak English when not on duty. Ester and Rosa refused to sign the pledge, but the other Spanish-speaking employee agreed. As a consequence of not agreeing to assimilate, the two women were fired. Their employers claimed that Ester and Rosa's refusal to sign the pledge essentially meant that they fired themselves.

The article is titled "Clash of Cultures Tears Texas City," and alludes to the cultural clash between the English-speaking employees and the Spanish-speaking employers. However, a more subtle and powerful cultural clash was missed. This clash was the one among the Latina women, who were of the same culture and spoke the same language but were pitted against each other. Ester and Rosa were pitted against the other employee who was favored by the employer because she agreed to stop speaking Spanish.

This story shows us how institutions foster divides among the neoindigenous, and illustrates how schools foster divides among the neoindigenous. The Latina worker who signed the pledge to speak English is in many ways like the student described above who sat quietly on his own because the teacher praised him for doing so. The employees who refused to sign the pledge are like students who either cannot or will not comply with the norms of the traditional classroom. In the long run, just as Ester and Rosa were pushed out of their jobs, the neoindigenous who fail to acclimate to the structure of school are pushed out of school. Most importantly, Ester and Rosa were thrown into conflict with their fellow Latina coworker in the same way the neoindigenous experience divisions in the traditional classroom.

As early as elementary school, students learn to associate certain behaviors with positive validation by the teacher. It is common practice in early education for the teacher to single out "model" students, saying things like, "I like the way that x student is performing x behavior," encouraging other students to follow suit (and shaming those who do not or can not). While creating norms in an elementary classroom may seem innocuous enough, it becomes problematic as students get older and certain behaviors are equated with "being smart." Thus, smart students who are loud, inattentive, less articulate, or who challenge the authority of the teacher (by refusing to perform the teacher's idea of smartness) are less likely to be compensated for their academic ability with good grades. The students who receive preferential treatment because of their performance of teacher-defined smartness become targets of ridicule by the students who refuse to perform, not because of any false notion of "acting white," but for being fake. Those who choose not to perform or cannot perform then enact behaviors that disrupt the flow of the classroom. Rather than perform smartness, they deliberately act out an exaggerated version of what the teacher has chosen not to recognize.

In this model, very few of the students end up successful. Those who perform smartness never truly engage in the learning process because they are too preoccupied with playing a role. Students who refuse to comply become so preoccupied with shattering the inauthenticity of the classroom that they lose the opportunity to be academically challenged. Students who actually manage to engage in the learning process become lumped in with the group of "performers" and never truly connect to their peers—which, in the long run, affects their self-identity as neoindigenous. This is why cosmopolitanism has such significance in urban classrooms.

Neoindigenous cosmopolitanism provides the educator with an alternate lens through which to view traditional teaching and its effects. It pushes educators away from separating out students based on preconceived notions of what "smart" looks like, and toward teaching as a community practice where no one student models the norm but, rather, every student shapes what the norm is. Students develop a connection to each other and to the classroom that is authentic and that values authentic representations of where they stand ethnically, racially, academically, and emotionally.

Developing a Cosmopolitan Ethos in the Classroom

In the traditional urban classroom, the teacher spends the entire academic year fighting against communal practices (certain ways of talking, moving, gesturing, articulating) that bring students together but which are seen by the teacher as disruptive. However, by the end of the school year, and as the pressure of teaching content to strict guidelines dissipates, the teacher eases up on classroom management and the classroom naturally takes on a more cosmopolitan feel.

Teachers often tell me stories about these magical moments they have with students toward the end of the school year that take them by surprise. The narrative is usually the same. There is the "tough" student who gave the teacher so much trouble who ends up being "amazing" at the end of the school year. Each time, the teachers wonder what created the shift in the student's attitude. In some cases, they even attempt to attribute the student's change in behavior to their instruction. One teacher once told me, "Maybe the student appreciated the tough structure of my class and just didn't have a way to tell me." My response was simple. If the student thought your "tough structure" was really a great way to teach, why did it take till that structure was loosened at the end of the year for the student to shine? What this teacher did was no different than what many other teachers do at the end of the school year. They start speaking to students like they are people, and even ask their opinions about what the class should do in terms of trips and end-of-year celebrations. When this happens, glimmers of a cosmopolitan classroom naturally emerge. In response, the students react differently and the teacher begins to engage them on a new level.

The goal for the teacher is to create a classroom environment where the same collective joy, celebration, and camaraderie that come at the end of the school year are present in the classroom throughout the academic year. This camaraderie is fostered when the teacher utilizes the practical tools for developing cosmopolitanism described below.

Speaking the Students' Language

The first practical tool of cosmopolitanism is the consistent use of language rooted in neoindigenous culture to support and reinforce the notion of a shared community. This language may originate outside the classroom, and the context may not necessarily be related to teaching and learning, but the educator must work to apply this language to activities completed in the classroom. This is accomplished by utilizing call-and-response in affirming unity among students in the class, reciting sayings that support collectively overcoming challenges, and using phrases that support being resilient in the face of both personal and class-shared obstacles.

In my own academic journey, hip-hop songs with themes of overcoming adversity and stepping up to challenges were the soundtrack to my engagement in activities requiring hard work. I often tell my high school and college students that I would not have been able to complete my dissertation without a popular rap song playing in the background, a song that may have had many negative themes but that motivated me to keep working hard or "hustling." Playing this song on repeat helped me when I needed motivation to keep working. As I nodded to sleep during late-night writing sessions with another student who was also working on his dissertation, I would speak the phrase *Every day I'm . . .* and he would respond by repeating the word *hustling*. That exchange, which is from the chorus of that song, would wake us from our slumber and allow us to work just a bit harder to get our tasks completed. The significance of call-and-response to the neoindigenous cannot be understated, since it is rooted in the ways they communicate within their communities. It is a beckoning call in times of war, a means to soothe in times of adversity, and a form of entertainment. By bringing it into the classroom and tying it to cosmopolitanism, it serves as a connector between in-school and out-of-school worlds and activates the students' connection to the classroom.

Within hip-hop, as in the black church, call-and-response is a prominent feature. Therefore, it is natural that the cosmopolitan educator uses hip-hop music as a tool to connect to youth, and as an archive of call-and-response phrases. For example, a classic hip-hop lyric like "Can I proceed?" followed by the response "Yes indeed" can positively transform classrooms. For example, if a teacher is delivering a lesson and stops to say, "Can I proceed?" and then waits for the entire class to respond with, "Yes indeed," this allows the students to feel a connection to the teacher (because of his or her use of the phrase) and to see that the teacher is concerned with ensuring that all students understand what is being taught. The fact that the phrase is from hip-hop allows youth to see that neoindigenous culture is welcome in the classroom and the fact that the phrase is repeated by all, brings the entire class together under the banner of hip-hop.

Another set of hip-hop call-and-response phrases that I have seen used in cosmopolitan classrooms are *All for one* followed by *One for all*, and *I will not lose*, followed by a repetition of the same phrase. *All for one* and *One for all* are used in cosmopolitan classrooms at times when a student is at the board solving a problem and feels like he or she needs help. The student who is solving the problem yells out, "All for one," and anyone in the classroom who is willing to help responds by saying, "One for all." The student who is having a tough time at the board then enlists the support of his or her peer. This process, where no one is allowed to feel inadequate and where peers are excited to support each other academically, is the anchor of true cosmopolitan teaching and learning. To extend this practice, and further welcome neoindigeneity in the classroom, the instrumental of the song "All for One" by Brand Nubian plays in the background as the students work together or come to the board to answer questions.

The phrase *I will not lose*, which was popularized by rappers like Jay-Z, has become a powerful mantra for the neoindigenous. It is repeated constantly in adverse situations outside of school as motivation for overcoming obstacles. I have witnessed situations where youth used the phrase to motivate each other in hip-hop performances and in sports competitions. Welcoming, and even modeling the use of this phrase, in the classroom (particularly during challenging academic tasks) helps to build upon and then utilize the resilience of neoindigenous youth. It also fosters a strong work ethic in the urban classroom.

Implementing Distributed Teaching: The Cosmo Duo

Another practical way that cosmopolitanism can be implemented in the classroom is through what I call the cosmo duo. The naming of this practice comes from cosmopolitanism (cosmo) and the fact that it focuses specifically on two students (duo) who work together to ensure that each of them can support the other in their times of challenge. Creating the cosmo duos involves the creation of a space where the expression of vulnerability in the classroom is not taboo, and where those who elect to express this vulnerability are not viewed as weak by their peers. The cosmo duo localizes the process of cosmopolitanism to two people, and then uses the students in this two-person group to generate a broader classroom cosmopolitanism.

The process is based on the belief that if two students ensure that they are both supported academically, and if these duos exist among students across the classroom (particularly if they are students who traditionally underperform in school), the possibilities for a classroom where youth are deeply committed to each other's learning are endless. The specific ways to enact the cosmo duo process are outlined in the following steps.

Invite students who have been a part of a cogenerative dialogue to create cosmo duos. By inviting students who have been part of the cogen group to partner together in duos, the teacher has an opportunity to get students who already have developed an interest in improving their educational experiences, and have developed a relationship to each other to model the practice. The invitation should occur after the students have participated in at least three cogen sessions, and have established a solid rapport with each other. The following transcript is from an actual invitation from a mathematics teacher who invited a student to become part of a cosmo duo, and can be modified for use in other classrooms.

> TEACHER: I've been thinking about how much we have gotten accomplished over the last three cogens, and I wanted to find another way that you guys can help me and each other make this class better. I figure that if you can work together in groups of two, you can really support each other better.

STUDENT A: Does this mean that we won't be having any more cogens? Are we switching this to just being all on us?

TEACHER: Not at all. I am going to keep the cogens going. It's working so well. I just want to add another dimension. What do you think of this process?

STUDENT B: Sounds like a good idea. Guess I will partner up with Joey and Sam can partner up with Jose.

One of the benefits of implementing the cosmo duo process with students from the cogen is that it is easy for students to partner up with a peer since there is usually an even number of students in this group. It is important to note that the cogens still proceed concurrently with the duos. This means that students partner to work together in the classroom to support each other's learning, but still engage in cogenerative dialogues with the teacher and a larger group (as described in the previous chapter) to help improve the instruction. Once these partnerships have been established, the teacher engages them in the cosmo duo process, as explained below.

Encourage students to disclose their strengths and weaknesses with regard to the classroom content (test-score averages, understanding of content, and general comfort with the classroom environment). This process can be somewhat challenging because students rarely like to admit to their weaknesses. However, if they are encouraged to consistently discuss their weaknesses along with their strengths, they become accustomed to sharing with their peers. For example, a student who says that he or she does not understand a topic discussed in class should be encouraged to talk about their strengths with other topics or aspects of classroom life such as time management or organization.

In some duos, both students may share the same strengths or weaknesses. In these cases, they are encouraged to not only work toward cogenerating ways to address their collective weaknesses but to find an additional partner outside of their duo to help them address the areas where they need assistance. Once the cosmo duos have been established within the cogen, and then expanded to include partnerships with other students in the classroom, students begin to ascertain that they are being encouraged to find ways that they can assist each other in overcoming their deficiencies beyond their duo.

Have students in the cosmo duo explain to the larger class how their partnership has been working for them, as a way to introduce cosmo duos into the classroom space. During this presentation to the class, the teacher should ask the students to describe what is working well for them, how often they partner outside of school to work on content, and any practices in particular that they routinely engage in. After students have given their presentation, the teacher can then re-outline the process and discuss the ways that the cosmo duos described by the cogen group can be enacted in the classroom. This process positions the practice as something that the students can enjoy and benefit from and not a task that the teacher is forcing on them.

The teacher then creates the context for introducing cosmo duos in the classroom. This is ideally accomplished early in the academic year, with the teacher giving low-stakes assessments on material that may not have been taught yet or on what students should have learned during the previous year. The teacher can tell students that their grades won't be affected by these assessments, that no one is expected to know everything, and that the point is simply to "find out where you may need some extra help before we really start teaching new stuff." Given the low-pressure environment the teacher has created, students are more likely to divulge their academic strengths and weaknesses, and the teacher can begin preparing them to work together in duos that foster classroom cosmopolitanism. Once the teacher has begun the initial assessments and gauged the classroom climate to the point where it is apparent that students are ready to fully embrace cosmo duos, the entire class can proceed with the following steps.

Have high-performing students partner up with lower-performing students, and create a space in the classroom where these groups can target their specific strengths and weaknesses. Education research indicates that this process runs most effectively when the teacher dedicates an entire classroom lesson to describing what a cosmopolitan classroom looks like. The teacher defines cosmopolitanism, talks about what it means in the classroom, why it is important, and how it counts toward how students are graded in this class. Then, the teacher explains the goal of creating cosmo duos and asks students to declare their expertise or lack thereof on a topic that was previously taught in the class or a previous assessment. The teacher can ask who got a certain set of questions correct on a quiz and who didn't, or who understood a concept that was just taught or who didn't. Once students have declared what they either know or don't know to the class, they can then volunteer to match up with each other or be matched by the teacher.

If need be, the teacher may select two students from the class (e.g., one who performed extremely well and one who performed extremely poorly on a classroom exam) and partner them together. After working together for a period of time, this team might then be asked privately if they are willing to present to the class how their partnership enabled them to support each other's learning (similar to the presentations by the cogen-generated cosmo duos). This process gives fellow students an opportunity to witness a new model of what the classroom could look like, one where disclosing one's academic challenges is not seen as a negative thing, and where working together to address challenges is the norm.

Support students in creating plans of action for maximizing their strengths and teaching the content to each other. Once the partnerships in the classroom have been created, students are asked to pick a spot in the classroom where they can sit with their new cosmo duo partners and create plans of action for how they can support each other. The classroom structure during this process should deliberately be different from the traditional classroom. Students are allowed to move their desks to different parts of the classroom, sit on the floor if they so choose, and even go into the hallway to confer with their new partners. While students who have engaged in the cogen version of the duos have already seen how this model moves from theory into practice, developing plans of action is an authentic process that all students can work on together.

As the students sit in their duos and work through their plans, the teacher visits each group and poses questions that help them to structure their process. For example, the teacher might ask, Are you going to meet outside of class? Do you have each other's phone numbers or Twitter handles? When or where will you meet? How can I help you with your planning? The goal here is for the teacher, through the questions that are posed, to support the students in acknowledging the power they hold to create situations where they can support each other's learning both within and outside of the classroom.

Let students know that those who are strong in content will have their test scores increased by the same number of points as their partner who is weaker in content. This next step in enacting the cosmo duos in the classroom focuses on giving grades and classroom credit for students who successfully help their peers do better academically. More specifically, if a student who had a test score of 55 on a test receives a grade of 65 after being partnered up with a peer who scored a 90 on the same test, the test score of the student with a 90 increases to 100. This means that the teacher has to create opportunities for students to have more than one opportunity to take classroom exams or new versions of old exams. For many teachers this is a challenge, because they have a flawed notion of the purpose of classroom assessments and grades. In a cosmopolitan classroom, the goal of the class is not for the students to be assessed so the teacher can discover who the top performer is. On the contrary, the goal of the cosmo duo is for all students to reach their academic and emotional potential. In this model, a student's every incremental increase on conventional forms of assessment is valued and rewarded within the classroom structure, either via higher grades, extra credit, or some other form of classroom recognition.

In order to sustain the power of cosmo duos over time, and allow them to truly transform teaching and learning within and outside the classroom, it is important for teachers to provide opportunities for youth to enhance, develop, and reenergize their commitments to these partnerships. More specifically, one day a month should be dedicated to sustaining the cosmo duos. On this day, youth sit in the class in their duos, are encouraged by the teacher and their peers, and get an opportunity to present what they have been doing to support each other's learning. This may also involve establishing new duos based on new needs the students may have. This reconfiguration considers the fact that just because a student is an expert on one topic does not necessarily mean that he or she will be an expert on another one. In addition, it is important for youth to know and see that everyone can be an expert and/or need help as the class moves from one topic to another. In the monthly cosmo duo class meetings, students share ideas, motivate each other, and reestablish action plans as necessary.

In previous studies I have conducted on cosmo duos, students from a New York City public school who initially were the ones being helped by their peers almost always showed a marked improvement in academic performance after being engaged in cosmo duos for at least two weeks. After this time had gone by, interviews and surveys showed that these students were more motivated to learn, more engaged in classroom discussions, and deeply committed to continuing the cosmo duo partnerships. They also spent more time preparing for lessons and studying for class in hopes that they would get the opportunity to be a part of future duos in which they took on the support or expert role.

The implementation of cosmo duos stands in complete opposition to the traditional corporate classroom. The traditional classroom focuses on individual success and singular outcomes rather than on the more complex but communal aspects through which the neoindigenous measure success.

Fostering Cosmopolitanism: Building the Classroom Family

For neoindigenous youth who are often from communities that suffer from a myriad of issues, one of the chief symptoms of these issues is the absence of the nuclear family. In the comprehensive academic research of Anne Pebley and Narayan Sastry, the effects of neighborhood, poverty, and family structure on educational attainment were studied. Their work, and other research on education and family structure, reveals that students from broken families are less academically proficient than their peers from more stable homes. Many interpret this research to mean that the traditional family model of mother, father, and 2.5 children propagated as the societal ideal is the only model of family that works. I argue that those who do not have this traditional family structure can benefit from what we know about how this structure supports the academic and socioemotional development of children.

For neoindigenous youth, the quest for some version of the socioemotional stability that comes from the traditional family is a chief piece of what drives them. In many cases, the quest for this stability results in their involvement in gangs or the development of pseudo families where they name their peers or others within the neoindigenous community as father, mother, or sibling. In my work with youth who have engaged in criminal/gang activity, they easily identify their gang or crew as a family that values them. These new configurations of family provide some version of a structure that has been destroyed by forces like the infiltration of drugs into neoindigenous communities and the targeting of the neoindigenous by the criminal justice system.

I have worked with many white folks who teach in the hood who frequently complain that parents of their students don't respond to phone calls or don't show up to parent-teacher events and conferences. Not only do these teachers blame parents for their own issues with students, when challenged on their ineffectiveness in the classroom they defensively argue that they weren't hired to be a parent to these students. This response shows a willful ignorance of neoindigenous realities. Many parents in urban communities are working multiple jobs, may not have access to transportation, and are subjected to deliberate sociopolitical efforts to break down neoindigenous families such as the targeted incarceration of black males and support systems that advantage single-parent families.

Sociologists like John Hagan and Ronit Dinovitzer have documented the deleterious impact of imprisonment on both families and communities. Other researchers, like Becky Petit and Bruce Western, have also established that black males are imprisoned at a higher rate and for longer terms for the same crimes than their white counterparts.[2] Given these facts, it is clear that there is a complex relationship between incarceration, the breakdown of the family, and academic achievement. In response, the cosmopolitan classroom focuses on providing young people with what they may be missing through a re-creation of family structure and the use of academic achievement as a shared-classroom family goal.

It is important to note that despite the very problematic activities of street gangs, many of these organizations present powerful examples of ways to engage young people and embody a cosmopolitan ethos within an organization. Consider, for example, a gang called the Decepticons, named after the villains in a popular 1980s cartoon, *The Transformers*. In the late 1980s and '90s the Decepticons were one of the most feared gangs in New York City history, and were responsible for a number of robberies and assaults across the city.[3] The gang was notorious for traveling in large groups and using hammers and box cutters as weapons when they committed their heinous crimes. Given the violence of the gang, its origins may seem surprising: it was formed by students in one of the city's "specialized high schools." To gain admittance into this school, students from across the city from all races and socioeconomic backgrounds had to pass an exam that measured their academic aptitude. However, once they entered the ethnically and racially diverse school, the students felt divided across race and class lines.

Many of the students who were from neighborhood schools where the cultural makeup was less diverse struggled to find an identity in a school that brought them all together because of their smarts. Over time, groups of neoindigenous youth in the school, from urban neighborhoods across the city, began to form connections to each other. As a now-forty-something-year-old man who was an original member of the gang recalled, "A lot of us black kids who turned Decept [Decepticons] were smart . . . We passed the test to get in [the school], but we were being judged by the teachers and the white kids all the time.

We knew we were just as smart as they were, but they made us feel dumb. They saw us as violent and angry. Guess they were watching too much news about crack in our neighborhoods or something. So we just all came together and showed them what violence and anger really was all about. It really just started with just having each other's backs in the school. Then we ended up creating a family. Then that family ended up turning into something a lot more dangerous."[4]

My study of the Decepticons uncovered powerful camaraderie among its members and a number of team-building rituals that could easily be seen as powerful teaching tools. Unfortunately, the camaraderie and rituals they developed translated into something dangerous for the Decepticons and the rest of the city because they were generated under negative socioemotional conditions. The teenagers who became one of the most feared gangs in New York began as very smart students who did not feel welcome in school, and who created a family that would protect them from the negative emotions they felt within a learning institution. Cosmopolitanism, when understood and implemented in the classroom, looks to re-create the family structure one would find in a street gang but in a positive socioemotional context.

The significance of creating a family structure surrounding educational success can be seen within the popular Posse program that has grown in visibility across college campuses in recent years. This program recruits high school students of color from socioeconomically challenging backgrounds with "extraordinary academic and leadership potential to become Posse Scholars."[5] These students are often from neoindigenous backgrounds, and become scholars in predominantly white institutions that look very different from the high schools and communities from which they come. The students are brought in to college campuses as a cohort and make connections to each other based on their similar ethnic, racial, and socioeconomic backgrounds. They attend events together, take classes together, and support each other in navigating the academic and social challenges of being away from home.

This program has been generally successful for students, and graduates a high number of youth of color. In many ways, the Posse program is designed to foster cosmopolitanism, and is not that different from the structure of the Decepticons. Students who are traditionally not accepted come together to build rapport with each other, and create a pseudo family. The major difference between the Posse program and the Decepticons is that the Posse family comes together under conditions of accepting and celebrating the neoindigeneity of the students and their contributions to the universities they are attending while the Decepticons were formed because the students did not feel accepted, were not celebrated, and wanted to respond to the pain they experienced.

A former high school student who ended up being a part of the Posse program captures the sentiment of being a young person engaging in cosmopolitanism perfectly when he says, "After leaving a gang and then being a part of a cosmopolitan classroom it is a feeling like you are part of something bigger than you that relates to being academically successful. Knowing that you have a community that supports you in being smart is the beginning of a whole new world opening up."[6] This student returned to his former high school during one of his college breaks to talk to students about attending college. He had been engaged in processes like the cosmo duos while he was a student, and the connections he had to his peers carried on with him even after he had been accepted to, and was doing well in, college.

In a speech to the entire high school, he mentioned that he easily could have taken a path that led somewhere other than college. He credited his success in school with being in classrooms where practices that supported cosmopolitanism allowed him to see himself as a scholar and a person who could do well in school. He mentioned that "before that, I was running in the streets with my 'family' the second I got out of school. Not like my mother and father family but my hood family. My crew." As the student described his search for a group that always "had his back" or would always be there for him, I realized that the cosmopolitan classroom family replaced his street family and led him to look at life differently. This is an experience that all of the neoindigenous should be able to experience.

Welcoming Neoindigenous Forms of Communication: The Handshake

A couple of years ago, after an Olympic men's basketball warm-up game against Brazil, President Obama met with the Team USA players and their coaches. At one point during the meeting, he shook hands with everyone present. He walked up to the mostly white coaches, who were lined up ahead of the players, and gave each of them a firm traditional handshake. This process continued until he got to basketball player Kevin Durant, who is black. To Durant, the president extended his hand much less deliberately. He swung it toward the basketball player's hand, pulled him in for a hug of sorts, and then slid his hand away in one fluid motion. He had given two distinctly different handshakes in just about a minute. Somehow each one was appropriate. What does the president know that many teachers don't about the power of nonverbal communication? I would argue that what the president knows is the ways that the neoindigenous communicate and the meaning behind gestures that go unnoticed to those who are not privy to the nature of their nonverbal modes of communication.

In every neoindigenous classroom where cosmopolitanism is established, the nature of the exchanges among students, and between teachers and students, are very different than they are in other classrooms. They are in many ways like the two handshakes I just described—intended to meet the same goals, but approached differently for different people. One of the chief indicators that you are in a cosmopolitan classroom is the complexity of nonverbal communication that is shared among those who are present. Where traditional classrooms focus on students raising their hands and waiting for validation from the teacher, cosmopolitan classrooms focus on free-flowing exchange and shared cultural practices.

Among the Decepticons, one of the most powerful forms of communication was the handshake. When members of the gang met, they exchanged elaborate handshakes that involved various hand rotations

and contortions of fingers that lasted minutes. The handshakes signaled a greeting, a celebration, an affirmation, and on many occasions, the nonverbal acknowledgment that two people or a group were
about to embark on a task together. I argue that if handshakes emerge
when solidarity is reached among the neoindigenous, then they can
be used to create or spur on moments of solidarity in the classroom.

Researchers have identified that touch is a significant form of
communication that can be associated with positive relational and
educational outcomes, but that if misperceived can lead to a number
of negative emotions.[7] Given the possibility of touch being either
negative or positive, it is important for the teacher to only engage in
practices that generate mutually positive emotions. I argue that an
educator who has created a special handshake to share with students
when they get an answer right can generate positive emotions because of the significance of the handshake in neoindigenous culture.

However, such an exchange can easily go awry with the neoindigenous if it is perceived as inauthentic. This signals to students
that there is a cultural divide in the classroom and that the teacher
represents the power wielder or "white folks." The classroom handshake should begin with the teacher extending the hand informally
to a student for doing something like answering a question correctly
in the class, and then, as the student responds, adding something
new like a fist bump. Initially, this will be awkward for a teacher who
does not understand the culture of the young people, but the teacher
should be persistent, perhaps saying to the student after the initial
attempt, "Let's try it again." When this action is repeated in front
of the entire class, students may laugh or even be confused by the
teacher's intention. The response from the teacher should be simply
to carry on with the lesson.

The handshake should not be given again until another student
in the class answers a question correctly. At this point, the teacher
extends his hand to the student and invites the class to suggest another hand movement that can be added to the existing handshake.
"The handshake" thus becomes something that the class constructs
together. While this practice may appear superficial, the process leads

to students being more attentive to and engaged in the classroom space. In many cases, students who laughed at the initial handshake become the ones who want to answer questions correctly so that they can partake in or add a new twist to the evolving classroom gesture. Before long, the practice becomes a ritual that the entire class enacts, building solidarity.

Fostering Family: The Classroom Name

The final practice supporting cosmopolitanism in the classroom is the naming of the class. Much like how the students from Brooklyn called themselves the Decepticons, and sports teams are known by their names in addition to their cities, the classroom should have a special name as well. I have given my classes names like the Physics Phenoms or Mathematical Magicians, which are very different from generic names like "class 904" or "middle school math." There are also mantras (like one-liners from rap songs mentioned earlier) that the class can repeat when anyone says the name of the class. These types of practices reinforce students' connections to their classroom and each other and help them forge an identity around the content being taught.

For the educator, understanding the significance of cosmopolitanism, and establishing norms that allow youth to create deep and personal connections to the classroom, elevates classrooms from places or locations of learning to spaces that have the potential to truly transform teaching and learning.

Cosmopolitanism calls for the recovery of humaneness in relationships among and within groups.[8] The practices outlined above may appear insignificant to teaching and learning when studied on their own. However, when implemented in the classroom, they can have a dramatic impact on the relationships between students and the teacher and between the class and the content.

CHAPTER 7

Context and Content

In the previous chapter, I wrote about the differences between Barack Obama's traditional handshake with a white Team USA basketball coach and "bro handshake" with black basketball player Kevin Durant. In previous work, I have written about when Obama "dusted his shoulders off" at a political rally, and when he and his wife, Michelle Obama, fist-bumped each other at a political event a few years ago. Most recently, after the horrific events in Charleston, South Carolina, in June 2015, when a twenty-one-year-old white man murdered nine members of a black church, President Obama delivered the eulogy for Reverend Clementa Pinckney, who was killed in the shooting. On each of these occasions there was a powerful signaling to the African American community that the president expressed.

In the case of the fist bump and the "dusting off of the shoulders," African American populations, and black youth in particular, were seeing gestures that the neoindigenous see on street corners every day. The use of those gestures by Obama conveyed the message that the president is "one of us." When he motioned with his hands as if dusting off his shoulders, he was signaling a connection to the rapper Jay-Z and familiarity with the song "Dirt Off Your Shoulder," making a connection to the neoindigenous youth who know that gesture well. In the eulogy he delivered, the president spoke with a very distinct cadence, with a unique set of inflections, and at the end invoked a call-and-response. These subtle adjustments in his speech may have gone unnoticed by some people listening to or watching the eulogy, but they were highly significant to attendees of black churches across the country, because Obama was in many ways speaking to them by using their own distinctive cultural cues.

Social Capital and Social Networks

Sociologists describe this shared cultural knowledge as social capital. Pierre Bourdieu argued, as many sociologists do, that people have shared forms of capital based on their similar backgrounds and experiences, and that they exchange this capital freely for their collective benefit when they are in particular social fields. The cultural capital may be generated in a shared social field, but may become enacted in another to increase one's capital. Consider the example of students in a classroom who have never met each other before but are from the same neighborhood. Because they are from the same neighborhood, and have had similar experiences within that social field, they develop certain forms of cultural capital that may help them to navigate the classroom. Without personally knowing one another, there are ways that they develop a shared response to a task the teacher may ask them to complete that they feel is too demanding or has no value. An eye roll enacted by one student may spark a head nod or another eye roll by another student, and before long, the entire class is communicating with each other without using words. The entire class has now increased its capital as connections are made throughout the larger group. These nonverbal forms of communication help students through whatever struggles they experience in the classroom. The context-based rules of engagement and modes of communication come into full display because exchanges of cultural capital are occurring.

When this type of communication is happening, and students are engaging with each other using a nonverbal language that only those who are from the same out-of-school contexts can understand, they are forming what the sociologist James Coleman calls "dense networks."[1] Dense networks are tight-knit and interconnected binds that human beings with shared social capital have to each other. In the case of the neoindigenous, these deep connections begin outside of the classroom as they share experiences, but then get solidified in classrooms where they feel threatened or uncomfortable and need solidarity with others to overcome the cultural divides that exist between students and teacher. Dense networks facilitate trust and cooperation, and depending on the contexts where these networks are fortified, can have either positive or negative consequences on those who are developing them.

For the neoindigenous in urban classrooms, their dense networks with each other are strengthened by their shared frustration with the structure of traditional classrooms and the difference between the context of the classroom and that of the world outside of school. For these students, when capital is exchanged and dense networks are created, there are benefits (such as the feeling of solidarity among the neoindigenous) that are gained. Unfortunately, there are also what sociologists Alejandro Portes and Patricia Landolt describe as "negative consequences" to being deeply entrenched in such networks.[2] These negative consequences are the outcome of being so tightly packed into, and reliant on, social networks that it hampers the willingness (and in some cases ability) to make connections to, or exchange with, people from other social networks and different contexts. For the neoindigenous, this means that opportunities to exchange capital with the teacher or the school may be lost. For example, they may choose to ignore the teacher or neglect tasks that they feel have nothing to do with their communities/contexts.

Similar to how social capital is exchanged within the dense networks of the neoindigenous, the school and people within it exchange their own forms of social and cultural capital and create their own networks. For white folks who teach in the hood who are deeply entrenched in the culture of traditional school/education, there are benefits such as being validated by their peers and the institution for exchanging solely within those networks. However, like the neoindigenous, they also have to deal with the negative consequences of these networks as they relate to their ineffectiveness and success as educators. The negative consequences of being too wedded to particular networks play out for educators when they fail to recognize the value of connecting to the contexts in which students are embedded. In my own teaching career, the need to expand my networks became clear during my second year of teaching.

After a generally unsuccessful first year, I decided to spend the second year of my teaching career at the same school where I had previously taught. I returned for the single purpose of proving to myself that I could be an amazing teacher in a school where I felt like I had barely survived the year before. On the first day of my second year, I walked into the same auditorium I had walked into the previous year, mentally prepared to teach differently. However, despite my best efforts, the first day of my second year was reminiscent of the previous year. The noise from outside the auditorium walls as the teachers waited for students to arrive was the same. The room had the same scent of fresh paint and old wood that paralleled the electric energy of the fresh teaching staff and old administration. Administrators whizzed back and forth in a dizzying way making sure that students were assigned to classes and teachers knew what they would be teaching. The school safety officers seemed frozen to the sides of the metal detectors at the entrance to the school, and a welcome sign on the auditorium door, recycled from the previous year, hung on by a thin piece of tape.

At one point, I looked around the room to identify some of my colleagues from the previous year and it sunk in how much the faces of my colleagues were different from the previous year. In particular, two of my colleagues who I had formed a strong bond with during my first year were not in the auditorium. The rumor around the school was that one teacher lost his cool toward the end of the school year and got into a fight with a seventh grader who insulted him. The other teacher decided that she wasn't going to have another year like the previous one and decided not to show up for her new class assignment. Unfortunately, no one in the school knew she had decided to quit until a week into the academic year. When she didn't show up to work, administrators called her home number, and she told them she had decided not to return.

Among the few colleagues who decided to return to teaching after the previous year was another teacher I had met on my first day. As soon as I spotted her across the auditorium, I walked over, smiled, and gave her a high five. I wanted her to know that the greeting was less of a hello or welcome back and more of an acknowledgment that I was glad she decided to stay. I was glad to have someone to work through the new academic year with, and after exchanging a few pleasantries and talking for a bit, it seemed like she wanted the same thing. We quickly began talking about how challenging the last year was, and how we both planned to be better teachers this year than we were the year before. We both felt like we had learned so much during that first year that we were ready to embark on a new adventure with our students. As we began to talk in detail about our plans for the new school year, a bell rang and students rushed into the auditorium. I rushed back to the group of seats where my class was supposed to meet me, and waited for my students to assemble.

The next day, I arrived early to prepare for my students and discovered the classroom across the hallway was already occupied. My colleague had gotten there earlier than I had, and she was placing student work from the first day on the bulletin board. I was astounded that she had given the students work on the first day, and that it was already graded and up on the board. Somehow this inspired me, and I decided to get to school early the next day. When I arrived to the school about an hour early, I saw she was already there. I was once again inspired by her dedication, and eventually asked her if we could work and plan our lessons together.

On some mornings, we were both the first teachers to get to the school. Most evenings, we were the last ones to leave. We both believed that if we spent more time planning our lessons in the mornings and organizing our classrooms in the evenings, we would be able to have better classroom management, get students to do better in our classes, and have a more successful academic year. She was much more diligent at this than I was. Somehow, she found the strength to arrive just a little earlier and stay a little later than I did. As the school year progressed, it became more and more difficult for me to devote the same amount of time and energy to my practice that I had at the beginning of the school year. Toward the end of November, I had gotten a sore throat that I attributed to not enough sleep and too much yelling. Getting sick had made me tired of early mornings and late evenings, and I felt like the effort I was putting into making my class better wasn't paying off. There was certainly some improvement in how prepared I felt, and the technical quality of my lessons had improved tremendously, but I still had to fight students to get them to engage with these well-planned lessons. Somehow, I hadn't convinced them to put as much effort into learning as I had put into preparing to teach. I was tired, frustrated, and felt that what my colleague and I were doing each day to improve our teaching was unsustainable and unhealthy.

One morning, after dragging myself into the school two hours before the day started, I walked into the classroom across the hallway and began to speak to my colleague about the challenges I foresaw with maintaining our classroom-planning regimen. As I explained, she placed her fist under her chin, nodded in agreement, and began to doze off. I raised my voice just a tad to wake her up without startling her, and she woke up talking about a lesson plan she was working on. I told her she had fallen asleep while I was speaking, and she denied it. She quickly changed the subject and mentioned that we would be able to do better if we came in earlier and stayed even longer after school. Her passion and dedication inspired me. I both believed her and in her, so I continued following the taxing schedule even though I felt like it paid very little dividends for my students in the classroom. Somehow, we began to share experiences, challenges, and expectations. We had developed a shared form of cultural capital and had formed a close bond or dense network to each other. It had begun to have negative consequences on our general well-being, but we were both unwilling to recognize.

Over the next few weeks, I watched her become sick and take her first day off in almost two years. I also witnessed the loss of her sense of humor, and watched her literally drag herself into work every day. As I witnessed her come apart, the realization hit me once again that there was no way that either of us could keep up the schedule we'd created and maintain our joy for teaching.

Lessons from the Basketball Court

One afternoon, while we were lesson planning and mapping curriculum after school, loud but joyous noises came through the slightly opened window and filtered into the classroom. Like on my first day as a teacher, I was drawn to the loud noises the students were making. However, instead of being intimidated by the ruckus, I was envious. Somehow, across the street from the housing projects, in a neighborhood that many would not deem a safe place to live, young people had found immense joy in living and playing. This was happening at the same time that my fellow teacher and I were working hard to teach them day in and day out, and robbing ourselves of this same type of joy. I walked to the window to watch the students dribbling a basketball and jumping rope as they moved toward the basketball court that was behind the school building. I looked at them curiously and then back at the stack of papers piled on the desk where my colleague and I sat designing lessons. In a heartbeat, I decided that I was going to go out and join the students on the basketball court. I'd love to say that my decision to head outside was based on some profound insight I had about the need to spend time with my students, but in truth it stemmed from jealousy—the students got to have fun and

I didn't. I had almost forgotten what it felt like to have fun, and I decided that I was going to enjoy myself for a change.

When I walked onto the basketball court, the students' immediately became defensive. One of them told me that they were allowed to be there and that I couldn't get them in trouble. I responded by picking up a basketball that had rolled over to where I stood and taking a shot. Before long, they realized I was just there to play. One student threw the ball back at me, and I took another shot that rolled awkwardly around the rim before it slowly fell through the net. The students giggled, and I challenged a young man who was on the court to make the same shot. He walked close to me, nudged me over, took the shot, and smiled as the ball fell through the hoop without touching anything but the net. He responded by saying, "This is my court. I hit nothing but net on my court."

The students and I ended up playing for a few hours. During the game, we talked about everything from the neighborhood to the lives of the students. The conversations were effortless, and we may have been there longer except for the fact that my colleague walked by on her way out of the building. As I left the court to speak to her, the students asked if I would be there the next day, and without giving it a second thought, I said yes. The moment that I was asked if I would be back the next day was powerful. It lasted just a few seconds, but it was the point where there was a break in the dense networks that both the students and I had developed with our respective groups. My dense network with the school and my colleague remained intact, and the students' dense networks to each other were still present, but at that moment we were somehow extending beyond them. The sociologist Ronald Burt identifies what was happening in that moment as weak ties that can give positive consequences.[3]

The next day, I walked to the basketball courts as soon as school was over in hopes of warming up before the few students from the previous day arrived. However, as soon as I walked onto the court, I saw that an army of students had arrived before me. In less than twenty-four hours, word had gotten out that a teacher had come out to play basketball. They had arrived to see if it was true, but also, unbeknownst to me at the time, to invite me into their world. Within the first two hours of playing basketball with the students, I was invited to a block party in the neighborhood the next weekend. After a few more afterschool games in subsequent weeks, I received invitations to breakfast, church, and a number of community events. Once I started taking students and their families up on these offers, I began to identify different phenomena across each of these settings that were significant for students' learning. As I spent more time in the students' communities, my social networks within the communities expanded, and I spent less time in the morning and after school planning sessions that used to take up most of my time.

I was learning about the students and enjoying myself so much that I didn't realize that I was still putting the same amount of time into my new activities as I was into formally planning for my classes. The lessons about the students that I was learning were plentiful, and I couldn't soak them in quickly enough. In one instance, as we played basketball in a local park within the housing project closest to the school, the students' deep social and emotional connections to *el blocke*, or the hood, became glowingly apparent. As we played, a student pointed out a memorial a few feet away that was created for a young man who had died of an asthma attack about a year before. It was clearly well taken care of, with candles and flowers adorning a graffiti art piece that featured the young man's face, as well as quotes from his favorite rapper. A year after the memorial was constructed, everyone who passed still bowed their heads to show their respects. In the same way that the indigenous see their land as sacred and develop cultural practices based on how they interact with the land, I witnessed the neoindigenous express a deep respect for their neighborhood and that memorial. I began to wonder what it would look like if a memorial like that was in the school. What would it mean to have the same spirit of respect and reflection pulled into the school while celebrating the life of someone who meant so much to the community?

The more deeply connected I became to the neighborhood where the kids came from, the more I began to understand the significance of context as a pedagogical tool. In particular, after the exchange below, I began to see how students would subsume their ethnic identities in a local one that was tied to their immediate context.

> RESEARCHER: Since we've been talking about our personal histories . . . let's talk about you kids. Where are you all from?
>
> STUDENT A: Me? I'm from 183rd Street and Walton.
>
> STUDENT B: I'm from Walton too, but like Fordham Road side. Like the other side.
>
> STUDENT C: I'm from Kingsbridge.
>
> RESEARCHER: Cool. But it seems that at least two of you are Latino. I mean, even your names are classic Spanish names. I was expecting different responses.
>
> STUDENT B: Oh, well, you asked where we're from. Like [long pause] my family is from DR [Dominican Republic], like we go to the parade on the concourse [a large thoroughfare that spans a few neighborhoods in the Bronx] and all that, but I'm from Fordham.
>
> STUDENT C: Right. I guess you could say I'm Puerto Rican, or Nuyorican, or whatever. I was born in PR, but I'm from the Bridge [Kingsbridge].

As each of these students described themselves as from a different place within a twenty-street radius, I realized that they were forming affiliations to each other based on their closeness to local geographic spaces and the networks within them. Students had weak ties to their ancestral places of origin and strong ones to networks within their neighborhoods. The more I began to understand these complex dynamics, the more I was challenged to create learning spaces within the classroom that looked and felt more like their neighborhoods. The question then became, how do I create classrooms that students are connected to in the same way that they are connected to their block or street corner?

The revelation of the significance of context to my teaching was powerful, and the first person I thought to share it with was the colleague with whom I had formed such a deep connection to around our teaching process. As we spoke, she seemed unconvinced that my "discovery" had any real meaning for us in the classroom. She asked how I thought playing basketball and hanging out with the students was time better spent than planning lessons. She talked about how much the students needed structure and had to pass exams at the end of the year. She spoke with much conviction, but my response to her was clear and simple: "Please just come to my class and see what's happening with these kids." She agreed to visit my class, and when she did, I saw her eyes light up as she saw students engaged, laughing, cracking jokes, and also learning. The air was light, questions about science came as naturally as quick conversations about sports and community events, and classroom management wasn't an issue.

When the class ended and students walked out, she remained at the back of the classroom and frantically took down notes on what she thought she had just seen. I asked to see her notes, and in response, she asked to see my lesson plan for the day. I shared the document with her, and she commented that there was nothing in my notes about how I got the students to react the way they did to the tasks I assigned. It was then that I began to share that the magic behind what she had witnessed was based less on sound lesson planning, and more on a new set of criteria I had discovered in my out-of-school interactions with students. I got students to engage with me and each other differently because I blurred the lines between the in- and out-of-school contexts. As she asked me more specific questions, it became clear that whether another teacher could re-create the dynamics that existed within my classroom depended less on my criteria for using context, and more on their willingness to embed themselves in neoindigenous contexts and generate their own ways to use context as a bridge to learning. Teaching more effectively requires embedding oneself into the contexts where the students are from, and developing weak ties with the community that will organically impact the classroom. Once I eased up on my lesson planning and delved more deeply into my learning sessions with students in their own communities, I picked up different aspects of youth culture, they interacted differently within my classroom, and I uncovered new approaches to teaching that drove my pedagogy.

On basketball courts, I saw the power of teamwork and friendly competition. Here, I also saw the beauty of communication through head nods and quick glances. The teams who won the most games and stayed on the court the longest had mastered the art of delivering nonverbal signals to each other. In a fraction of a second, a wink and quick head nod transformed into an alley-oop dunk that would cause an opposing player to fall to the floor in utter embarrassment and confusion about what just happened.

These same nonverbal cues were evident during card games I was invited to when I visited students' homes. In churches, I saw the impact of call-and-response and music. On street corners, I saw the effect of colorful murals and handshakes that signaled a sense of community, and everywhere, I saw how different contexts impacted the way that people interacted with each other. The more I observed these practices and saw how students responded in different contexts, the more I referenced them in the classroom and allowed them to become a part of classroom practice.

Learning to Use Context

To ensure that what I was learning from the neoindigenous went beyond my classroom, I invited my colleague to join me on my next visit to the community. During this process, it became clear that there are three basic steps to fully learning about, and engaging with, students' context. It is important for the educator to take all three steps in order to move toward a better awareness of how to meet the needs of the urban student and teach with youth contexts as an anchor of instruction. The first involves being in the same social spaces with the neoindigenous, the second is engaging with the context, and the third is making connections between the out-of-school context and classroom teaching.

With regard to the first step, reality pedagogues understand that there is no more effective way to develop social networks with the neoindigenous than to immerse oneself into their communities. While formats like the cogen serve as ways to begin dialogues with students, coteaching gives youth agency to participate in the teaching, and cosmopolitanism helps them to feel like the classroom is a place where they can express vulnerability, reality pedagogy does not kick into high gear until the teacher becomes a presence *beyond the classroom* and in the community. While the process of leaving the school (where one is in a position of authority) and going into the community (where one is not) may seem daunting, it becomes easier if the process is embarked upon slowly and cautiously. I argue that the place for teachers to start is in businesses that are in close proximity to the school and are patronized by students. These places are usually where students spend much of their time before and after school and are public spaces where the teachers' presence would not be particularly odd or unwelcome.

After visiting the places where youth spend time around the school, the next step for the educator is to begin visiting places that are farther away from the school and closer to the home communities of the students. This includes places of worship, housing projects, and other local gathering points. In the case of my colleague, we went on what I call a "hood tour" of the community that her students were from. This was not a trip to observe them like they were zoo animals, but an opportunity to be with, and learn from, the students. With my colleague, we began just by being on "the block." We walked throughout the neighborhoods and observed all that was going on around us. As she became comfortable with being outside of the school building, and being farther away from it, we moved onto the second step of learning/engaging with context.

This second step requires hard work once one is within the context. When I engaged in this process, I spent hours asking students in-depth questions about what I had observed to ensure that my reading of the experience was authentic. I read the nonverbal cues among the basketball players, then asked them about these cues, and practiced them until I knew what they meant and could anticipate they were coming. I knew on some level that having this information would make me better equipped to interact with students in the classroom, and I reveled in the joy and wonder of the experience.

For my colleague, the first step of just leaving the school and being in the context was tough enough. The part of the work that required engaging in neoindigenous practices was even more challenging. She could not see the direct benefit of the experience, and therefore could not justify the reasons to engage in the part of the learning that required harder work than just being there. My experience with her led me to conclude that this process can either be painful or enjoyable depending on the perception of the learner. My colleague could not make an explicit connection between working hard in the community and being prepared to teach. She found the task of interacting with youth and possibly breaking a sweat on the playground while playing basketball or jumping rope with students as not being worth it. On the other hand, I chose to enjoy the process. I went home on certain nights a little sore from playing with a group of teenagers, embarrassing myself a few times on the court or turning the rope for double Dutch too fast or too slow, but I believed the social and cultural capital I was gaining from these interactions was worth it.

For anyone who has an interest in learning something, it quickly becomes clear that the process requires a time commitment to activities/tasks that may be challenging. When the activities or tasks that one is engaging in on the course to receiving an education are something that the learner sees as valuable, the entire process of learning becomes pleasurable, and the student experiences what researchers have called the "joy of learning." I argue that there is an equivalent "joy of teaching" that must be reached and that this joy comes from being so embedded in the same context with young people that you are operating in the same place and space as they are as you exchange information. With the neoindigenous, this type of education can be witnessed as they work tirelessly to become experts in performing certain rituals that make them experts within their community. For example, the time, training, and physical activity required to be a b-boy (break dancer/dance performer) within neoindigenous communities is extraordinary and can be viewed by an outsider as being too taxing. However, for those who are engaged in this activity and take pleasure in learning more about to how to fully engage in the culture, the hard work is pleasurable. Explaining this to my colleague required reminding her of what she described as a "powerful lesson" that she saw when she visited my classroom and convincing her that there was a direct correlation between the time I spent actively engaging in the community and the time students spent actively engaging in my classes. The students were working hard in my class because they had come to enjoy learning there as much as I enjoyed learning from and within their contexts.

The third step in the process of educating the neoindigenous is to make connections. In this case they are being made between what is learned within neoindigenous contexts and the content one is required to teach. This is the part of the work that allows the educator to truly fulfill the role to lead students to learn something new or see the world differently than they did before they walked into the classroom. I argue that this part of the three-step process (making connections) is what my colleague and I were attempting to do all along in our early-morning and after-school lesson planning without the tools for truly doing it effectively. We were planning lessons without having the contextual information that we needed to make the planning truly effective.

For example, we would spend hours pulling different questions from textbooks, planning transitions between classroom activities that would keep students engaged, and bouncing ideas back and forth about how to get students to pay attention to what was being taught. We would consistently try out these newly discovered ideas or experiments about teaching, they would fail miserably, and then we would spend more time researching as many new approaches as we could, based on studies, standards, and curriculum. I came to realize that instead of going through this process, I could go directly to the students' contexts and simply work to make connections between what I observed and the content I was charged to deliver.

This marriage between content and neoindigenous contexts allows the teacher to circumvent the tensions that come from the cultural misalignments between school and community. For example, when students have developed a disdain for school because they feel that to be successful they must repress their authentic selves, making them see that the content being delivered respects and values their culture makes them feel like the classroom is not at all like the rest of the school. The classroom that respects their contexts becomes a way to reconcile the broken relationship the neoindigenous have to schools and schooling. When a teacher makes connections between the context and content, innovative lessons that connect things like graffiti and mathematics or hip-hop music and science begin to emerge. The specific types of lessons will vary depending on the unique neoindigenous contexts that the students are from but will each connect to students from specific contexts in ways that the traditional curriculum cannot.

This third step of connecting context to content also involves the use of artifacts from the places youth come from as the anchor of instruction. These artifacts can either be symbolic or tangible, but each is necessary for completing the final step of this aspect of the work. By symbolic artifacts, I am referring to things like phrases or terms the neoindigenous use in specific spaces, gestures/hand movements that have a deeper meaning, and descriptions of things/people/phenomena present within urban contexts that cannot be physically moved from the places where they were created. Tangible artifacts refer to objects that the teacher brings in from neoindigenous communities that students can see and touch in the same way that they would be able to in their out-of-school worlds. For example, rocks or plants from a local park will have more significance in the biology classroom than pictures from a book or from the Web. When students can physically see and examine these artifacts in the classroom and are also able to interact with them once they leave the school, the divides between the school world and their real lives are bridged. In addition, pictures of street signs, store fronts, building facades, graffiti art, and other parts of the students' communities can be used in classrooms to explain subjects that range from mathematics to history.

Being able to appropriately utilize context is one of the most valuable skills a teacher can have. It is a skill set that can easily be learned and can make up for other major deficiencies in classroom practice. For example, a teacher who lacks expertise in classroom management but who identifies an artifact that has some cultural significance to the neoindigenous will engage the students in the classroom so that managing the classroom will not be an issue. Convincing my fellow teacher of the value of connecting content to context required working together to identify artifacts I had collected during my work in the community and planning lessons based on them. As she engaged in this process, she found lesson planning to be quicker and easier. She didn't have to spend hours on end designing lessons or coming up with examples that the students would respond to because they came naturally and quickly. The next discovery was that students responded more positively to these "new" lessons than to any of her previous ones. This revelation prompted her to burst into my classroom when our students were in the cafeteria, beaming from ear to ear about the amazing lesson she had just taught. She shared with me how refreshing it was to have students really listen to her, how much learning was happening in the classroom, and how her mathematics lesson, in which she had used various pictures of elevators in housing projects, had led to a breakthrough in her students' understanding of geometry.

How Context Affects Content

When context is infused into instruction in a way that truly reflects where the students are from, a new challenge emerges: the teacher has to be more knowledgeable of the content than ever before. When the students are fully engaged, their curiosity about the content is awakened, and they are constantly exploring the connections between the context and the content that the teacher identified and brought to the classroom. Once this happens, they begin asking questions that go beyond the scope of the traditional lesson. They begin to ask why and how things are happening and begin drawing connections between the content and other abstract concepts that the teacher may not have previously thought of.

In some instances, once students are fully engaged, they begin asking questions that are either outside of the expertise of the teacher or that require very specialized knowledge about the subject. For example, the students in the geometry class mentioned above began to ask questions about the origins of geometry and where the decision to use certain shapes in urban construction came from. These were questions that the teacher was unprepared for, and had never learned herself. These questions were posed with a type of unbridled enthusiasm that led them to jump out of their seats, raise their voices, and wave their hands wildly. This enthusiasm could have very easily been misread as an unwillingness to adhere to the norms of the classroom, and the questions they were asking could have been misperceived as attempts to distract the teacher. In the past, when students displayed this type of behavior, the teacher misread it as evidence that the class was not going well. She would raise her voice, get the students to be quiet, and then continue on with following the lesson plan that she had spent so much time developing. However, during this lesson, and as a result of the work that she had done with understanding content within the neighborhoods that the students came from, she mentioned that she was able to allow students to fully express themselves, and noticed that the class never got fully out of control as she would have previously anticipated. She remembered seeing them raise their voices on the basketball court and still execute plays. And she saw them supporting each other in rap battles in the neighborhood. So she allowed them to express themselves.

When the class in its exuberance diverted from her lesson plan and students began asking questions that she was not prepared for, she simply acknowledged to the students that she didn't have answers to their questions. One student responded by saying, "But you're the teacher. How come you don't know?" This became the perfect opportunity to share with them that just because she was the teacher didn't mean she had all the answers. Students then listened attentively as she explained that she was going to try to answer the question about the origins of geometry based on what she knew, but that the entire class could research the answer together for homework. She later described the learning space she created that day as "the most powerful classroom lessons ever." She was "in the zone, and so were the students," she shared with me.

This type of lesson—where the teacher and students are occupying the same place and space while discussing and learning content—occurs when there is what the French sociologist Émile Durkheim described as "collective effervescence."[4] In the neoindigenous classroom, collective effervescence is reached when the joy of teaching matches the joy of learning and a truly cosmopolitan space is created. In these spaces the level of rigor is elevated, the number of higher-order questioning escalates, and the discussions about the content often reach levels that surpass the knowledge of any single individual in the classroom.

In preparation for this type of class, and to ensure that it happens regularly, there are four steps the teacher can take to prepare. The first is to learn to welcome nontraditional ways of expressing content knowledge. The second is to create a space in the classroom for youth to post the questions they have that may go beyond the scope of the teacher's knowledge or what is being taught. The third is to provide extra credit/grades for students' expression of content in nontraditional ways or for researching questions their peers are posing, and the final one involves creating a space where both the student and the teacher are learning content together.

The first step of allowing content to be taught on an optimal level is to welcome nontraditional ways of expressing content knowledge. This requires an understanding that when students are keyed in to the instruction and have a personal investment in learning, the teacher will "lose control" of the class. It necessitates an acceptance that students will speak in nontraditional ways that may include slang and/or expressions that are not traditionally accepted in schools. Therefore, the very notion of controlling the class has to be dismissed. The optimal teaching context for content to be ideally delivered is one where the students are so excited about learning the content that their responses to the teaching are visceral and cannot be controlled or quantified. Furthermore, in a classroom where there is collective effervescence, the exchange of information will be so fluid that the students are bringing their full selves (which include their neoindigenous language and expressions) to the classroom. When this happens, the exchanges between students and the teacher keep elevating until a point is reached where the teacher will not know the answers to students' questions.

It is at this juncture when the collective effervescence of the classroom can be threatened. This happens when the teacher seeks to reassert his or her authority in the classroom as the center of knowledge. In other words, the teacher tells the students to quiet down or stick to the topic at hand in an effort to bring the lesson back in line with their prepared plan. In other scenarios, where the visceral responses to being engaged in the lesson play themselves out as students raise their hands wildly or stand up in excitement, teachers may seek to regain control of the class by addressing "behavior," silencing students and moving them toward a "more normal" classroom experience. This type of reaction to active learning (what I call the students' approach to learning) counters whatever efforts were made to align out-of-school contexts to content and defeats the opportunity for content to become a shared form of social capital in the classroom. This means that the teacher must work purposefully to allow for disruptions in the traditional sanitized classroom by welcoming the often loud and irreverent responses indicating deep student engagement.

Earlier I described the black church as a space that can provide a model for teaching. In these spaces, even within a structured church service, it is acceptable for church members to "catch the spirit" and express the euphoria of being within a space that allows them to fully express their emotions by moving, walking, singing, and dancing with reckless abandon. In the classroom, the equivalent of catching the spirit is the collective effervescence that is reached when the teaching is free-flowing and unbridled. The teacher has to fight the urge to stop the student from "catching the spirit" around the content.

The second step of allowing the content to flow freely is a tangible and easily implementable step. It requires creating a space in the classroom like a wall or bulletin board that is explicitly dedicated to having students post questions related to the content that they are thinking about, or that the teacher or his or her peers couldn't answer. To raise the level of rigor in the exercise, students should always be encouraged to ask questions not only that they want answered, but also that can stump the teacher. The only requirement for writing on the board is that whatever is asked has to be related to the content being delivered.

Students should know that this space is also available for those who may not be as verbal as their peers, and who need a platform for posing questions related to the content to their peers and the teacher that they may not feel comfortable asking in class. Many have called this type of space a parking lot—where participants in a social field can pose questions or share thoughts to be addressed later. In this iteration I refer to it as a "W board" because whatever is shared in that space should be a question (who, what, when, where, and why), not a declarative statement. I choose this practice because once the question is posed and then posted in the space, the rest of the class is responsible for finding an answer to the question. The teacher has to encourage students to research and find answers to questions, and then post responses to the questions back on the W board. This practice creates a physical space that promotes going beyond the content and elevates the discourse.

This leads directly to the third practice, which directly connects to the two mentioned above. When content is allowed to flow freely in the class, students should be compensated or recognized for both posing questions and responding to each other's questions. Students who are engaging in the class in nontraditional ways and especially those who write questions that make it to the W board or choose to answer them should receive extra points on exams, final grades, or, if the question or answer is particularly brilliant, a test score grade. In classes I have taught, students have answered questions from the board in more detail than I had ever imagined, and received up to twenty points on a test grade for doing so. Again, in order for a teacher to show a student that he or she values something, it is important to not just tell students, but show them—and one of the ways to do this is by giving students good grades for their nontraditional efforts.

Once context and content are focused on in a way that challenges how educators look at the communities where the students are from and the ways they allow youth to engage content, the very nature of teaching and learning begins to shift. This shift will challenge the comfort level of the educator and perceptions of what a "good classroom" looks like, but allows them to experience the true joy of teaching.

CHAPTER 8

Competition

The event had been planned for months. The elders in two warring neighborhoods had decided to end an ongoing feud in the only way they knew how. The elders convened and decided that there was going to be a battle. For the outsider to neoindigenous culture, the word *battle* conjures up images of violence and bloodshed. For the neoindigenous, the word means being a part of an event where one has to be at his or her mental, physical, and spiritual best and prepared to be challenged.

The battle is anything but physically violent. It is a place of confrontation, but also reconciliation. All who have had a part to play in any existent tensions are present so that the shared space they occupy can be cleared. The warring groups meet on common ground, look each other in the eye, settle the score, and most importantly, celebrate their commonalities. During the battle, the root of the tensions are unearthed, and this unearthing leads toward a solidifying of the connections among groups that may have been lost over the course of living and breathing in a world that profits from creating and sustaining divides among people. The elders understand that the root of many divides among the neoindigenous (such as those between ethnic and racial groups and among neighborhoods) is sustained by gun companies, media conglomerates, and even local businesses that profit from these tensions. The elders understand that the youth are pawns in a game to fatten the pockets of those who profit from their divisions, as well as their academic underachievement. They also understand that outlets like the hip-hop battle allow neoindigenous youth to move beyond infighting and division and toward deepening the bonds they have to each other.

The battle is an event that the elders push for whenever a disagreement threatens the psychic space that is needed for the youth to grow up feeling self-actualized and aware of the humanity of their fellow man. Because the process of preparation for battle is intense, it distracts from everyday concerns and helps the neoindigenous spend their energy on sharpening their skills instead of infighting. In many ways it combines leisure, spirituality, and a refocusing on shared culture, and provides healing. The battle therefore serves as an example of the ways that indigenous populations deal with stressors introduced to their lives by the dominant culture.

In a powerful article about the ways that aboriginal populations deal with health stressors, researchers looked at the ways that a particular indigenous community finds ways to cope by engaging more deeply in neoindigenous practices.[1] In other words, the chief way to address stressors created outside of the community is to delve deeper into the culture and utilize it to address the larger issues. This is why the battle becomes such a significant piece of neoindigenous culture, and why spaces between battles are important. Given the cultural divides between the neoindigenous and traditional schools, schooling becomes a stressor that the neoindigenous must endure, even though it inflicts tremendous symbolic violence on them. Symbolic violence refers to "the violence which is exercised upon a social agent with his or her complicity"[2] and is not necessarily a physical violence, but a socioemotional one where one's spirit is broken as a result of the constant pressure to adhere to a structure that runs counter to one's worldview. The chief way that both the neoindigenous and indigenous deal with these stressors is to delve back deeply into cultural practices like the battle.

One can see versions of the battle within indigenous and neoindigenous cultures across the globe. In Brazil, it plays out in capoeira—a martial art described as both a game and sport by participants in it, and a worldview by students of it, that often spills into competition. In capoeira, complex moves that combine kicks, spins, and other movements into contortions of the body are performed in a *roda* or circle, with onlookers from different backgrounds and skill levels watching two artists engage in a battle of sorts with each other. While the two people at the center of the capoeira performance or competition are against each other, they are in many ways also performing together. Author and martial artist Capoeira, who has the same name as the art he practices, describes capoeira as a response to the fact that life is a struggle and battle, and "the player sees that capoeira is teaching him to dance within and during this fight."[3]

The facing of an opponent becomes a means to strengthen the physical, spiritual, and mental self and recognize that the battle is not with the person who stands in front of you but with life. Capoeira beautifully describes the power of the battle as a "body dialogue without fixed rules or clearly fixed borders, where both violence or beauty may appear—often a mixture of the two—[wherein] the apprentice faces the most savage and brutal aspects of his comrades and himself." The discovery comes that one's comrade is no more violent than the world and that within the violence is a dance rather than a brute physical confrontation. In capoeira the kick or blow may come within inches of the body of an opponent, but no actual impact is made.

Ruth Stone, in a powerful edited volume on African music, showcased examples across the continent of Africa where competitive dance and performance serve as "the battle."[4] The nature of competition is a piece of indigeneity. One can see it in Tunisian saber dances, when men perform in competing pairs; the Sebiba festival in southeastern Algeria, where entire sections of a town with rival lineages engage in stylized battle, and the West African talking-drum circles, where drummers compete. With the neoindigenous, the tradition continues in the hip-hop battle, which is in many ways reminiscent of structures one finds in indigenous populations.

Neoindigenous Communities and the Hip-Hop Battle

In preparation for the hip-hop battle, the elders choose two warriors carefully after recommendations by the rest of their respective communities. The selection process is an elaborate community affair and consists of a number of intense smaller battles where winners show that they are skilled enough to represent the larger group. During this process, everyone in the community demonstrates how prepared they are for battle by showcasing their skills for the rest of the community. They suspend their affiliations to each other for the purpose of allowing the decision of who will represent the community in the larger battle to be as fair and as possible. These smaller battles look like the larger battles and consist of similar processes. Like in the larger battle across groups, two warriors in the smaller battle engage in a war of words. They perform raps consisting of sentences that rhyme but also complex metaphors, analogies, stories, and words. The elders study these smaller battles closely, and every person showcases their skills to the best of their ability because they want to earn the right to represent their community. In each of these smaller battles, a winner is chosen and then pitted against other winners. This process continues for as long as necessary until the entire community is convinced that they have identified the best person to represent them in the larger battle.

After this person has been identified, there is a brief celebration before intense preparation for the battle begins. Although only one person is selected to represent each community, the preparation process is a communal and time-consuming one. The time-intensive nature of the preparation for the battle benefits both communities in very subtle ways. First, it distracts each community from the tensions that led to the need for the battle in the first place. Second, it sharpens the skill set of the entire community as they prepare, watch, and learn from each other. Finally, it restores a sense of pride in self and community that may have been lost in the course of engaging with institutions that look at neoindigeneity or hip-hop culture as a deficit rather than an asset.

The chief activity of the warrior selected for battle is to engage in intense and rigorous research on the competition. This process is so detailed that it rivals and in some cases surpasses the process required to engage in traditional academic site research. It requires the warrior going deep and sometimes undercover into enemy territory in attempts to uncover hidden facts or details about how the opposing warrior and his community live. While going through this process, the warrior takes mental and actual notes on the observations made in these places. This process also entails deep studies of the technical aspects of the opponent's style of performance. The entire research process could take months and often includes assistance from others within one's group who can engage in the research process together with the person who was chosen to represent them. As this process continues, there are members of the group who are engaging in their own research on their representative. Once the entire community has sufficiently engaged in the process of gathering research on both their opposition and their representative, the next phase of the preparation process begins.

This next phase is a full rehearsal for the final battle. This process consists of sparring with others within the group who have also been engaged in the research process. Many of these individuals have been researching the warrior who will represent them and also the competitor from the other group and are now prepared to prepare for battle by bringing the best they have to offer through their research and their rap skills to the sparring sessions. In this process, the humanity of the neoindigenous emerges as the entire community goes through much effort to ensure that the warrior is sufficiently prepared for battle. Their belief in the democratic process of the selection of this representative allows them to support this person at the expense of their time and efforts. After each battle in this sparring phase, they give suggestions and share ideas. They all band together to build the arsenal of the warrior so that this person's skill set is at its height. In the process, they all become more skilled and prepared than ever. During the sparring process, they hear glimmers of the rap that will be performed during the final battle and become familiar with excerpts of it. The performer doesn't disclose too much of what will come until the day of the final event, and this secrecy builds anticipation for weeks until the day of the battle.

The day of the final battle is a celebration. The tensions among people from communities that were at war just weeks before have dissipated and been replaced with a shared excitement that builds to a crescendo until the two selected warriors appear on stage in front of everyone. Members of their respective communities flank each warrior, and then the battle begins. The battlers perform raps that showcase the best of their lyrical ability merged with the information they gained from research, ideas cogenerated by other members of their communities, and sharp delivery that is intended to emphasize the lyrics in the battle but that would be read as aggression in any other place but the battle. During the process, the rappers go back and forth until it is clear to everyone in attendance who has displayed the best combination of knowledge, technique, and ability. Once this happens, the rappers shake hands, members of their respective groups do the same, and the battle is over.

The events that build to the final battle are a collection of powerful moments that have the potential to transform classrooms. The battle is a contemporary form of indigenous modes of teaching, learning, and community building, and a way to engage in a teaching and learning process that is different from the one that inflicts symbolic violence on the neoindigenous. Most recently, rap battles have made a powerful resurgence within neoindigenous communities as mainstream artists have begun to attend and participate in battles that have aired on pay-per-view channels on national television. In particular, battle rap brands have emerged across neoindigenous communities in the United States, each generating thousands of loyal observers and participants. Despite this fact, the battle is rarely, if ever, discussed in academic settings. In response, I argue that we view the steps toward the final battle through a pedagogical lens and begin to identify the aspects of the battle that educators can bring into the classroom. More specifically, bringing the battle into the classroom helps neoindigenous youth heal from traditional teaching and concurrently helps teachers to approach competition in the classroom differently.

Bringing the Battle to the Classroom

The unique rites of passage within neoindigenous communities during the battle serve as powerful models for how to make youth central to the operation of the classroom. During the battle, younger members of the community are introduced to the norms of the larger social group by watching and then doing. They aren't schooled on the technical aspects of the battle but are allowed to challenge each other in preparation for the final event. They are also deeply engaged in the research process, allowed to play, fail, and watch at any point in the battle process without any serious personal repercussions, and then witness what it looks like to perform on the highest level as they share the stage with the warrior in the final battle.

This process helps us to reimagine how the neoindigenous learn. Rather than employing the traditional model that makes learning a passive process where the student learns in a sanitized way that is hyperfocused on writing or studying, I suggest that educators implement a teaching and learning model that positions novices as no different from experts. This process allows everyone to learn by doing while creating a space where a novice who is particularly talented can immediately become seen and validated as an expert. By implementing this model, the individualistic and competition-driven nature of traditional schooling is replaced by teaching and learning that creates cultural learning experiences. This is significant because the brand of competition that the neoindigenous engage in runs in sharp contrast to the competition that is found in traditional schools, where the goal is for one individual to be better than all others without a focus on building or supporting community or being successful together. When the neoindigenous enter classrooms guided by a form of competition that is foreign to them, they are once again faced with a form of symbolic violence that inhibits them from fully engaging in school.

Many teachers intuitively use game formats like *Jeopardy* to get students excited about reviewing or relearning a massive amount of information quickly. The game is a variation of the popular television show where contestants pose questions to answers that are on a board. The classroom game usually has groups of students in the class in competition with each other posing questions that match up to answers to topics the teacher has taught or that the class needs to review. Teachers choose this game because it allows young people to test their knowledge, review information, and compete as a group with other students in the class while everyone learns.

Whenever I deliver lectures or workshops to teachers, I ask if they've ever played *Jeopardy* with their students, and when they have used this game structure. In almost every instance they say yes, and almost always say that they play the game with students to help them prepare for standardized exams or major tests. When I ask how students respond to the competition, the teachers mention their enthusiasm and motivation. In response, I've always wondered why this approach to instruction is only used right before an exam and not taken as an exemplar of good teaching practice that can be used throughout the year. I argue that this is the case simply because a strategy that encourages enthusiasm and motivation does not align well to the existing approach to teaching. It does align rather auspiciously with the structure of the rap battle. Teachers who play *Jeopardy* with their students often do so at the expense of possibly being reprimanded for being off schedule or not sufficiently rigorous. Despite this, they play the game anyway because they know that students are more engaged and are enjoying learning.

Bringing the concept of the hip-hop battle to the classroom accomplishes this goal as well. The only significant difference between out-of-school battles and in-school battles is that the former are focused on the subject that the students are learning and on research about the academic particular content. Students respond to the challenge of focusing their raps on classroom content with the same enthusiasm they do when battling outside of the classroom, and take advantage of the space that is created for them to showcase their academic and hip-hop skills.

A Model for the Classroom Battle: Science Genius

An example of how the battle is brought to the classroom is a project I recently conducted across science classrooms in three cities. Science Genius B.A.T.T.L.E.S. (Bringing Attention to Transforming Teaching, Learning, and Engagement in Science) is an initiative focused on utilizing the power of hip-hop music and battle culture to introduce youth to the wonder and beauty of science. The core message of the initiative is to meet urban youth who are traditionally disengaged in science classrooms on their cultural turf and provide them with the opportunity to express the same passion they have for hip-hop culture for science. This focus on science was decided upon based on the fact that it is among the subjects that youth are most disengaged in and where achievement gaps persist. Furthermore, it is one of the subjects that are most representative of approaches to teaching that silence students.

The project began with a very simple first step that can easily be replicated across subject areas and across schools. This step involved going into classrooms and asking teachers to suspend whatever form of assessment they intended to use for the present section/unit. Instead, they were asked to give all students the assignment to write a rap or poem about the content they were learning. Students were then told that they would be graded on the assignment in much the same way that they would be on a traditional assessment. This process is equivalent to announcing the battle and letting the entire community know that anyone can toss their hat into the ring and showcase their skills, though not every person decides to enter into the battle. In much the same way, not every student will engage in the task to write a rap or poem about the content, but those who have not found success within the traditional school structure are often eager to engage. Once students understand that they have an opportunity to showcase their neoindigenous knowledge with the content, they are told that there is another class or school that will be engaged in the same task and that the raps will result in a culminating hip-hop battle. For youth who are deeply embedded in hip-hop culture, hearing that there is a battle instantaneously calls forth their neoindigenous traditions and further motivates them to research and study their content. In preparation for the final battle, youth become deeply devoted to the research process.

In the science battle I developed, I added a few layers to the process mentioned above for the purpose of allowing students to understand that the academic rap battle is not an attempt to co-opt their culture, but an opportunity to bring their culture into the classroom. This included partnering with a respected rapper who had an interest in education and the subject being taught, expanding the battle beyond one school and into other schools across the city, having young people from neoindigenous communities who were recent graduates volunteer to be in the classroom on a regular basis serving as a broker between the culture of students and the culture of the teacher, and planning for a final battle across schools (with direct input from students on how the final event was organized). These layers added a level of authenticity to the project that propelled youth into actively engaging more quickly.

I find that teachers can replicate these same processes if they make an honest attempt to validate neoindigenous culture. In many cities I have worked in, inviting a local rapper to do volunteer work in schools is a simple task that only requires making a phone call to a local radio station or doing an Internet search to find the artist's agent. In fact, getting a local artist that the students admire is just as effective as securing a more popular rapper. In fact, a local artist has more significance to the students than someone who is not from their community but who is more popular. In the case of securing community volunteers, reaching out to a local college or university department in education will often result in a number of volunteers to support the educator in organizing the battle within their classrooms.

However, even in the absence of a rapper or volunteers, simply proposing and implementing a classwide or schoolwide battle will result in the engagement of students and a more complex understanding of the subject/topic being taught. Through the classroom battle, it immediately becomes apparent to the teacher that is not familiar with the nuances of youth culture that that there are dramatically different ways of expressing knowledge about content.

Once students have engaged in the battle, and have become deeply entrenched in the content being taught, the teacher has created the space for the students to be able to fully engage in the content. Youth who are deeply embedded in hip-hop showcase their knowledge in ways that go beyond reading and writing and include expressing their content knowledge orally. In hip-hop, the highest level of orally presenting information is through the art of the freestyle. The freestyle is an aspect of hip-hop culture where participants in the process share all of themselves through a given method like rap or dance in an impromptu fashion. The rap freestyle often involves a person rapping over an instrumental with an impromptu rap without much structure. It is a lighthearted activity that is often used as an opportunity for youth to sharpen both their rapping and content skills for when they actually write a rap or song. The process involves thinking on one's feet about content and then presenting it to an audience through words and the exercise of the mind rather than what has been prewritten.

Presenting one's brilliance through words instead of written text has been part of the tradition of the neoindigenous for hundreds of years. Consider the story of Thomas Fuller, a slave who lived from 1710 to 1790 in Alexandria, Virginia. Fuller was described in his obituary as a man who could not read or write but "had perfectly acquired the art of enumeration." Fuller, despite his being illiterate, had the ability to complete complex mathematics problems on the spot and engage in scientific calculations.[5] In a world where specific forms of expressing knowledge and testing are privileged at the expense of other forms, Thomas Fuller would not have had what it takes to be successful. This brilliant man was precluded from being seen as a brilliant mathematician and scientist. What I find most striking about the Thomas Fuller story is the ways that he was able to orally express the brilliance that he did have. I argue that his ability to present what he knew right off the top of his head showcased an ability to freestyle. I often imagine Thomas Fuller being challenged on his mathematical skills by other scholars who could both read and write. I see them writing down questions and calculating with pen and paper to get their answer while he used the only tools he had, and that most of the neoindigenous youth in schools today have, which is their brilliance and ability to speak their knowledge. I see Fuller shocking them with his mathematically accurate answers much in the same way that I see youth in classrooms expressing their brilliance when given the opportunity to showcase this brilliance through rap and poetry. I then imagine the sparks that would fly if two people with Thomas Fuller's brilliance could face off against each other in a mathematical or scientific battle based on a specific concept they had each prepared for.

Each day, as we teach the neoindigenous, we have the opportunity to allow the modern-day Thomas Fullers to fully actualize their potential. However, in classrooms across the world, there are Thomas Fullers being silenced. It takes reality pedagogy and pedagogical strategies birthed from neoindigenous practices like the battle to bring their voices to the fore and allow their brilliance to flourish.

CHAPTER 9

Clean

Change the World and Dress Well Doing It

For young people, the first few days of school involve much more than entering a new class and adjusting to new teachers. For neoindigenous youth, that first week is a fashion show. Students show up to school to unveil new hairstyles and fresh haircuts, show off new school clothes or (more typically although less discussed) outfits from the previous school year revamped to look new.

While the wearing of "new school clothes" is a common practice across geographic settings and socioeconomic backgrounds, it exists with particular intensity and nuance among the neoindigenous. These youth are more reliant on artistic forms of self-expression than their counterparts from more privileged settings or backgrounds. In fact, the more challenging their socioeconomic backgrounds, the more sophisticated and unique their aesthetic tastes. Furthermore, the less engaged in modes of aesthetic expression one is, the less value and social standing one has within the neoindigenous community. For example, a person who does not understand the significance of a designer belt worth hundreds of dollars being worn with an inexpensive white T-shirt could not possibly comprehend how the person who is wearing this outfit sees the world or learns in school. This person does not have the insight into neoindigeneity to understand that the wearing of luxury goods/items with other "less valuable" articles of clothing simultaneously celebrates and mocks high fashion and creates art.

This is a phenomenon that plays out in many communities where there is economic inequity. Consider, for example, the Sapeurs, members of the Société des Ambianceurs et des Personnes Élégantes, in the Congo. These are working-class men who live in one of the poorest countries in the world but embrace a colorful sense of style and art in their clothing. These gentlemen, who live in the shadows of their French colonizers, cannot afford to indulge in the world of luxury that the upper classes have access to. In response, they create their own unique style of dress that adopts and then refashions products made for and by the most affluent. Sapeurs will match a luxury item they have come across with clothing made by a local tailor and create their own form of brilliance. Like the neoindigenous, when the Sapeur catches a glimpse of what those who have power see as a status symbol, they will pursue it with reckless abandon. Even small status symbols like a pair of sunglasses can become a hot commodity when infused with cultural significance. For the neoindigenous, there are many examples of how a lack of resources manifests itself in creativity and originality in style and aesthetics. This striving to make oneself look better off than one is, and to demonstrate a culturally aware fashion sense, is brought into the classroom and affects how teachers interact with students.

Walking in Our Students' Shoes

I vividly remember an experience a few years ago when a first-year teacher, who had been recruited by a program that brings college graduates from affluent settings to teach in urban schools, approached me after a speech and asked if she could talk with me about a student she was having a hard time reaching in class. She told me that this student had several different pairs of new sneakers and would match his baseball cap and clothes to his footwear. She also mentioned the student's sister, whose outfits were always perfectly coordinated and who "even had matching beads in her hair." She then described a specific outfit that this student had worn to school the previous week, and stated that she couldn't understand how a family who qualified for free lunch could spend so much time and money on clothes. In response I asked her how she thought a family with so little could afford *not* to feel good about themselves and dress well. It was clear to me that this teacher's inability to connect with her student stemmed from her lack of understanding of neoindigenous culture.

I wondered how it was possible that a person charged with the responsibility of teaching urban youth could have so little grounding in neoindigenous culture. But it wasn't my intention to judge her. I knew that she was sincere in her desire to reach her students, and I knew it was important to give this teacher something tangible that she could do once she got back to her school. I suggested that if she truly wanted to reach that student, she should pick up a nice pair of sneakers and a cool jacket that the students would admire. Confused and visibly upset by this response, she said that she thought I was there to help her and not make jokes at her expense. I gently explained to her that I was not joking, but she turned away from me without saying a word and disappeared into the crowd.

I attempted to follow her to assure her that I was not making fun of her, but I quickly lost sight of her. I was sure that she was as offended by my suggestion as I was by her clueless description of the student and his sister, but my intent was not to offend and my suggestion was genuine. For days, I played back our interaction in my head until about three weeks later when I received an email from the teacher. In the email, she mentioned that she had always heard her students making fun of her sneakers but she had ignored them because she didn't really care about clothes. She mentioned that after she spoke to me, she realized how much she did care about what her students wore. She had seen that there was some connection between what she was wearing, what her students wore, and her success as a teacher, and she was willing to take my suggestion. She closed her email by telling me she planned on buying a new pair of sneakers, in the expectation that this would make her classes better.

I emailed her back: "Please understand that my suggestion was not just about buying new shoes, but more about being aware of the power of wearing something that symbolizes something aesthetically significant to the students. Please do not expect that just by wearing certain sneakers your classes will be automatically better, and please realize that if you buy the wrong pair of new sneakers, you will not be any better off than you were initially. In fact, with the wrong pair of new sneakers, you may be in an even worse position than you were before. What the sneakers do is open up a portal to a new type of conversation that has the potential to transform your instruction."

After that email, we remained in communication about issues related to teacher bias, and how her misunderstanding of her students' culture was at the core of her struggles to connect with them. In our email exchanges, she told me about her purchase of a popular pair of basketball sneakers, and her experience walking into the classroom wearing them for the first time. She mentioned feeling a connection with students when she walked into the building that day, and immediately being pulled into a conversation with students about what she was wearing and why she bought them. She described "feeling euphoric as students I had never spoken to recognized me." She asked, "Is this what the kids feel when they get all dressed up?" She was beginning to see that the focus on attire was more than just what one was wearing; it was about the feeling that came with it.

Because of our conversations about how to make the students feel like she was not being condescending or mocking, she was able to tell students that she bought the sneakers because she saw them on some students and liked them. She wanted to learn from them and so she picked a pair that meant something to them, and also something to her, because she liked the colors and they matched the bag that she carried to work every day. She shared with the students that she'd spent a lot of time on her selection. Her thoughtful response drew her students to her. It opened up the space for them to give her suggestions about other things she could wear, music she should be listening to, and this spilled into transforming the classroom environment. It also opened up the space for an honest appraisal of how the classroom could better support their learning. By wearing those sneakers, she came to understand the value they held and what they represented. She also came to see the emotional significance that art and dress had to students. Finally, the sneakers were a password that let her into a new dimension of students' lives that allowed her to understand the power of their style, art, and general aesthetics.

While many may not see what style has to do with teaching and learning, I argue that the art of teaching the neoindigenous requires a consideration of the power of art, dress, and other dimensions of their aesthetic. Teachers often fail to understand that the bleak realities of urban youth and the drab physical spaces they are often confined to contribute to an insatiable desire to engage in, and with, artistically stimulating objects and environments. The wearing of the matching outfits and the euphoria that comes with being recognized for one's self-presentation serve as an escape from a harsh reality. For example, while many consider graffiti to be an indicator of urban decay and expressions of gang territory, the reality pedagogue understands that it is much more than that. We see it as an indicator of being in a space where youth have a strong desire to express themselves artistically and an opportunity to take advantage of a cultural artifact that speaks to young people because it is created by them. Graffiti is a way for the neoindigenous to dress up their neighborhoods in much the same way that clothing dresses up the body. Each graffiti piece can be seen as the equivalent of placing a rose in one's hair or placing a handkerchief in the pocket of an otherwise drab suit. The art that is created by graffiti artists highlights and accentuates the beauty of who and what exists in the neighborhood.

The role of the educator is to utilize artifacts like graffiti and phenomena like fashion consciousness to invoke an emotional connection to the classroom. This is done through the creation of a curriculum that explicitly focuses on themes like graffiti and fashion and then uses them to deliver content. Reality pedagogy involves a critical deconstruction of all phenomena that exist within communities and that have an emotional connection to the neoindigenous. This positions art and aesthetics as central to teaching and learning even though they are too often relegated to being extracurricular. Reality pedagogy functions with the general principle that the work of raising rigor or guiding students to think more deeply is achieved through identifying phenomena that emotionally connects or motivates the student, and that the most significant emotional connections we have are to the art we consume[1] and the most powerful and healthy emotional releases we have is through this art we create.[2]

The teacher must work to present himself or herself as respectful of, and willing to engage in, parts of the artistic world of the neoindigenous that schools seek to make invisible. One way to do this is by learning to dress the part. By this I mean that engaging with an audience who values aesthetics requires attention to one's attire. This does not mean that teachers have to dress like someone half their age or completely transform who they are and what they look like, and it does not mean that dressing like students will automatically make one a better teacher. However, the incorporation of neoindigenous fashion along with the teacher's own style serves as a powerful jumping-off point for rich dialogue with youth that opens up the space for powerful teaching moments.

This is particularly the case for teachers like the one I described earlier who are apathetic when it comes to expressing a personal style through dress. These are people who will blindly question a student's choice to wear new and expensive sneakers because they themselves choose to wear the same pair of shoes until they get a hole in them. For those who have the luxury of not being concerned with how they look or dress, it can be challenging to appreciate how and why it means so much to others. Teachers may come from enough privilege or wealth that they have no need to be concerned about how others view them, they may be a part of a subculture that necessarily avoids care about one's attire as part of a larger political statement, or they may be genuinely uninterested in their appearance or how they are perceived by others. Each of these groups of people have a privilege that many of the neoindigenous do not because they do not live in a world where they are judged by what they wear and do not need their body to be a canvas for self-expression like the neoindigenous do.

have found the stark similarity between the two places to be painfully obvious. In a school I visited in Detroit, which was a short car drive to a correctional facility, the look of the school and the prison was so similar that I was convinced that the same contractor completed the construction of both buildings. Everything from the metal detectors one had to walk through before entering each building to the tile in the bathrooms and the framing around the bulletin boards was eerily similar. If one were to consider the bars on the windows in the school and the bars on the prison cells, or the teachers yelling like wardens, the similarities between the school and the prison would be even more powerful. The question is then, how are youth expected to truly engage in the classroom when even the physical structure and aesthetics of the places where they are supposed to be learning are the same as those in places where they go when they have been arrested?

In a recent study that consisted of a series of interviews with youth across urban settings about their experiences in classrooms, my research team uncovered many powerful reasons for neoindigenous engagement in and disengagement from school. In the study, we visited schools weekly and then interviewed students after class in a classroom that currently wasn't occupied, and that they took classes in. We chose these classrooms because it was convenient to be able to ask students about a classroom that they were just in, and we assumed that interviewing students in these classrooms (where they spent significant amounts of time) would make them feel comfortable and also more likely to give answers to our questions. As we visited schools, arbitrarily selected classrooms and posed questions to students about their school experiences, we noticed that many of them would give very short and quick responses to our questions. In response, we would ask more in-depth follow-up questions in hopes that we would be able to get more information from students. In most cases, our efforts to get more in-depth answers were futile. However, on occasion, we would go to certain classrooms to interview students and would have no issue with getting students to answer our questions. These students would be elaborate and descriptive in their responses and gave us all the information we asked for. This confused many on the research team because there appeared to be no rhyme or reason to how and why we would get amazing in-depth responses from some students and close to nothing from others. We asked them all the same questions with generally the same group of people.

Weeks after the interviews, we combed through hours of videotape and made a fascinating discovery. In the classrooms where students gave more in-depth responses, we found that there was evidence of inclusion of neoindigenous forms of artistic expression in the classroom. In one classroom, there was a wall painted in blackboard paint where students had written their aliases and nicknames in graffiti letters. In another, regular classroom posters were complimented by posters of famous hip-hop artists and quotes about hard work and resilience from everyone from contemporary rappers to classic philosophers in a graffiti-style font. We believed that we had stumbled on something powerful, that the more artistic and aesthetically inclusive classrooms seemed to make students more likely to respond to our questions. To test this theory, we began to invite students who initially did not answer in much detail within their classrooms to be reinterviewed in the classrooms that that reflected neoindigenous art and culture. In each case, students took more time to answer our questions and responded in much more detail. When we asked students why they responded differently than they had before, they mentioned that they were more comfortable during this round of interviews. In one instance, a student even apologized for how she had responded during the first round. "It just felt like regular school," she stated. "It was like I was going to get in trouble so I had to watch my back and not say much." Because we had conducted interviews within classrooms with a traditional structure, she felt like the interviews were being conducted to implicate her in some wrongdoing rather than to solicit her opinion.

The unexpected outcome of this small research study led me to look at the physical classroom environment more closely, with the aim of understanding how the neoindigenous experience symbolic violence in certain classroom environments and come alive in others. This led to an identification of a number of tangible practices teachers can implement in order to foster the neoindigenous aesthetic in classrooms. The first is to allow youth to express their sense of style or fashion without being reprimanded for it. In fact, as long as their way of dress does not get in the way of teaching and learning, there is no reason why young people should be punished for what they wear. This recommendation is difficult for many educators who believe that it is part of their responsibility to "prepare youth for the workforce or adult life." Many teachers hold on to this belief about their responsibility despite the fact that the most successful people in the world today do not have a uniform or require their employees to have one either.

In schools across the country I have witnessed and heard stories about students who get "in trouble" because they refuse to take off their baseball caps. In some instances, the refusal to remove the baseball cap escalates to the point that it leads to suspension from school. This happens because schools do not realize the significance of the baseball cap or other neoindigenous attire to neoindigenous culture. Educators spend so much time fighting for a rule that was established because of an old adage about gentlemen removing their hats that they don't stop to think that it has no significance in contemporary contexts. The question for educators to ask themselves when it comes to enforcing rules about neoindigenous forms of expression is simple. Does the fact that the student chooses to do/wear this have any impact on my teaching, their learning, or his/her intelligence? If the answer is no, then that form of self-expression should be welcome in the classroom.

Having made this point, it is important for educators to let students know about how people in other contexts may perceive them based on their attire, and the many options they have in responding to the biases of others. The work of the teacher is to welcome youth forms of expression, and then be clear and frank with them about what the rules of engagement are in the world beyond the classroom.

Choosing not to welcome the artistic and aesthetic dimensions of neoindigenous expression makes the teacher complicit in contemporary forms of oppression against neoindigenous students and their culture. Forcing youth to ascribe to a way of being, existing, and appearing despite the fact that it runs counter to who they authentically are is reminiscent of the historical practice of forcing indigenous Native American populations to cut their hair and dress like Europeans as part of their education. Historian Lonna Malmsheimer presents images of Native Americans at the Carlisle Indian School from 1879 to 1902 that portray them as stripped of any expressions of indigenous culture.[4] Numerous photographs from that era show "before and after" images of indigenous populations in native dress and then assimilated to white norms. The work of reality pedagogy in urban schools seeks never to replicate these colonizing processes but rather to ensure that the neoindigenous aesthetic is welcome in the classroom. To make sure of this, all the teacher has to say is, "In this class, you can be whatever you want to be and wear whatever feels comfortable for you. As long as we do our best academically and prove to the world that we are more than what we wear, how you dress is up to you." Students respond to this statement in powerful ways, free to bring their full selves into the classroom.

Another way to consider the aesthetics of the neoindigenous is to create a graffiti wall in the classroom. This is a place where youth are allowed to write and draw freely on the wall. In classes where this has worked best, the teacher identifies a wall and paints it with blackboard paint. Youth are then allowed to use chalk with different colors to create murals, draw, write their nicknames or "tags," and exchange messages with one another. Allowing for this space in classrooms not only makes the class more attractive, but serves as a therapeutic space for students.

Finally, and perhaps most importantly, the teacher must show respect for neoindigenous artistic customs by engaging in them in a significant way. This work can easily be perceived as either mimicry or mockery, but it's neither. This work entails a recognition of what the aesthetic cultural expression of the neoindigenous is, and then seeks to engage in or with it rather than merely observe and exoticize it. This is partly why I suggested to the teacher discussed earlier to wear something that the neoindigenous would appreciate in order to show some connection or respect for them. In working with urban youth of color, it's important that we show respect for their unique customs, much as we have come to do with the indigenous. Consider for example the historical practice throughout the 1800s and up until the 1950s in some places of "human zoos" where the indigenous were treated like zoo animals and put on display to be ogled by spectators as they wore their indigenous apparel.[5] In these zoos, the goal was to showcase the indigenous and their culture. At times, it involved placing them in an exhibit next to apes or other animals and observing them and their culture (including dress) like it was something subhuman. In many ways, when we objectify youth and observe their culture without entering it or participating in it, we implicitly carry on a tradition of subhumanization. This type of interaction with the indigenous is the opposite of the work of anthropologists and other researchers who (despite the problematic phrase) knew that it was important to "go native" in order to do any work with the indigenous.

Educators who work with the neoindigenous should be willing to immerse themselves so deeply into the culture of the other that the cultural embeddedness manifests itself in the clothing one wears and the aesthetics one adheres to. I am suggesting that the teacher does not stop short at watching the students, but takes the steps to fully engage so as to express their connection to, or learn about the purpose of, the neoindigenous choice to dress a certain way. The work here is for the teacher to gain insight into the nuances of indigenous identity that includes a recognition that "cloth is one of the most important commodities used in the construction of identity"[6] and that for both the indigenous and the neoindigenous, "costume is language . . . because the future belonged to [indigenous] societies which were trifling enough but also rich and inventive enough to bother about changing colors, material and style."[7] The effective educator attempts to speak the language of the neoindigenous as it extends to cultural expression. In attempting to speak this language, its complexity emerges, fostering appreciation and respect on the part of teachers that supports their connection with students.

CHAPTER 10

Code Switching

Some of the most successful people in the world have an uncanny ability to fit in across multiple social settings. They read the codes or rules of engagement in a particular social field, identify which ones have value, adopt them, enact them, and through this process, form powerful connections to new people. In a previous chapter, I discussed the ways that President Obama signals to certain groups, a social skill that academics have called being a social chameleon or code switching. Code switching is a practice that has taken root in fields like linguistics, sociology, and cultural anthropology, and that focuses on where and how a speaker alternates between two or more languages or dialects in the context of a conversation or interaction.[1] In many ways, being a code switcher requires the same process as being a social chameleon. The major difference is the explicit focus on language by scholars who study code switching.

After reading through the philosophies and practical suggestions for engaging the neoindigenous outlined in my work, and for educators, administrators, and scholars who have gone through taking the steps outlined in this book, there comes a point where there is a search for the next step in this work. After making sense of the philosophies behind reality pedagogy, and implementing tangible pedagogical strategies like having students teach, giving them roles and responsibilities in the classroom, visiting communities, changing the aesthetics of the classroom, and enacting the various other techniques that challenge the ways they have been trained, the natural question to ask is what happens next? I am often asked questions such as, What is the goal of reality pedagogy after neoindigenous ways of knowing and being are brought into the classroom? How do we ensure that neoindigenous youth understand the dominant language and rules of engagement? Is it enough that they start enjoying their classes now if they aren't ready for the "real world"? My first response to these questions is that my goal is to have students become fully actualized. This may mean different things for different students. Some will leave the classroom feeling like their culture is worthy of being considered academic or intelligent. For others, this may mean that the classroom provides some affirmation of their beliefs about themselves and their intelligence. For others still, it may be that the class facilitates their starting to make associations between a particular subject that is being taught in a class and what they want to do with the rest of their lives. Self-actualization can never be assessed in the moment. Its dividends are paid decades after the class is over. The one thing that we do know is that it can only be triggered in a place that values the codes that students bring to the classroom.

I follow these types of questions with a reminder of the basic premise that guides all of this work. The students have to first connect to a classroom/school that welcomes their brilliance, celebrates it, and makes them realize that they have a natural ability (by virtue of their neoindigineity) to be academically successful.

I then make the point that students must be taught to become code switchers, social chameleons, and instigators/catalysts of the new norms in the world through the development of new and powerful hybridized identities. To validate the codes of young people in the classroom and then fail to arm them with the tools they need to be successful across social fields is irresponsible; students must use what emerges from the enactment of their culture in schools to help navigate worlds beyond the classroom that have traditionally excluded the neoindigenous. The work laid out thus far must be complimented with teaching youth the art of the code switch and its utility in their own neighborhoods, and in places beyond.

Navigating Multiple Spaces

For reality pedagogues, teaching code switching is concerned first and foremost with how we teach youth to be deliberate in a literal movement from one world with certain rules of engagement and language to another. For the neoindigenous to activate the beauty of the chameleon effect that comes naturally in new social fields they must first be deliberately taught to code switch. However, a distinction must be made between code switching and teaching students to be unnaturally like others for acceptance. When one becomes trained to be someone other than who they are, they become disingenuous or inauthentic and cannot develop what I call hybridized identities— where an individual can embrace and express many cultures with their multiple codes seamlessly and simultaneously.

Take, for instance, the new crop of urban "prep schools" attended by youth of color whose chief goal is to replicate the prep school model of elite and culturally monolithic affluent white prep schools. In many of these urban schools, students are taught to dress, talk, act, and behave in ways that are in opposition to their neoindigenous identities. They are encouraged to separate themselves from their neoindigenous culture in order to "make it out of the hood" rather than celebrate what their histories, neighborhoods, and home communities have to offer. These students then spend their entire lives copying another person's culture and looking down on their own. They see themselves as valuable only when accepted by the people they have been trained to see as valuable. In many ways, this model of schooling is a contemporary version of the Carlisle Indian Industrial School discussed earlier. Within it, successful teaching becomes a process of creating students who look and act like white affluent prep school students, and both teachers and students are rewarded for being able to wipe out any hint of their neoindigeneity.

This process of rewarding the neoindigenous for "being like white folks" is so pervasive, it even occurs within neoindigenous families, some of whom regard it as the ultimate mission in life. Some see blending in with white culture as a way to protect themselves against the violence directed at the neoindigenous. Recently, in light of a number of deaths of black people at the hands of white police officers, and the shooting of black teenager Trayvon Martin by a vigilante neighborhood watchman, a narrative has been created that black youth provoke acts of violence against them by dressing or acting in ways that reflect neoindigenous culture.

I argue for an authentic code switching that involves valuing oneself and one's culture while appreciating and understanding the codes of other cultures. It involves fluidly navigating multiple spaces and, in the process, creating new codes that embrace a more hybridized identity.

One of the most powerful code-switching exercises I have used in classrooms was developed by Bryan Brown, a professor at Stanford University who focuses on discourse in science teaching and learning.[2] Within what Brown calls the whole discourse approach, the teacher recognizes how certain words/terms/expressions convey meaning or describe concepts differently depending on where one comes from. In other words, many words and expressions can be used to describe the same concept, but only particular ones have value in specific contexts. The whole discourse approach recognizes this fact, and provides an opportunity for conversational language to be valued while introducing youth to new words that may be outside of their lexicon but that have the same meaning. The process involves creating a classroom chart that includes words used in both informal and formal settings. Youth then learn how to navigate between the two.

Privileging Neoindigenous Language

I have expanded on the whole discourse approach by introducing neoindigenous language to the process. The language chart includes categories for the different contexts/worlds that students may have to code switch between. This includes conversational/traditional

English, a subject language like science or history, and the language of the neoindigenous. What is so valuable about this type of chart is that it recognizes that there are different worlds, each with their own language codes, that students need to navigate across and between.

Once the chart is created, the teacher can then engage in a conversation with the class about the categories on the chart and the contexts in which certain words or expressions are accepted. This then leads to populating the chart with words or expressions that describe a single concept that could be described in multiple ways. Over time, as the chart gets filled in, students develop a more robust vocabulary. An example of what a beginning whole discourse chart looks like can be found below.

English	Science	Slang
Light	Photon	Lyte
Shine	Emit	Bling
Entire	Surface area	Whole joint

In this example, the words *light*, *photon*, and *lyte* (a vernacular spelling of *light*) are presented as having the same meaning. So are the words *shine*, *emit*, and *bling*. Despite the fact that these words have the same meaning and may be used to describe the same scientific concept, their use is limited to particular contexts. This means that if a student begins describing what happens to a leaf during one of the steps of photosynthesis, the statement "The sun gets lyte and blings on the whole joint" would be conceptually accurate and correct. If another student said, "The light shines on the whole leaf," that student would also be correct. Finally, if a third student said, "Photons are emitted on the surface area of the leaf," that student would be correct too. The difference between these three answers then becomes when and where each would be most appropriate.

In order to teach youth to code switch, I argue for a combining of the whole discourse approach with what I call "imagination exercises," where the class engages in a practice of imagining they are in contexts where only certain discourses are allowed. In this exercise, the teacher sets an imaginary context and the students and teacher practice the language and codes necessary for that context. For example, in the case of the different words used to describe the steps of photosynthesis, there are very specific locations where a statement like "It was getting lyte and blinging on the whole joint" would be privileged. Therefore, the teacher's responsibility is to establish the appropriate context in the classroom and then to validate it.

The teacher could say something like the following to the class: "I want you all to close your eyes for a minute and imagine that you are on a bench in the middle of the park next to your apartment building." As the students' eyes close, the teacher activates the students' imaginations by saying something along the lines of "Can you see the basketball players on the court? Do you see the kids riding their bikes back and forth? Now, one of your friends walks up to you and asks you about photosynthesis. For the next ten minutes, we are all in the park together. Open your eyes. What do you say to your friend who asked you the question?"

By painting this picture for students, the teacher brings their home lives into the classroom. Furthermore, their local colloquialisms and codes are welcomed in this space. For the next ten minutes, the teacher encourages students to talk in their neoindigenous language. Street slang is celebrated. The following exchange happened in one classroom during this ten-minute exercise.

> JOSE: So, basically, the laws of motion was a dope concept. Newton was just basically tryin' to explain why everything in the world was poppin'. Ya'll feel me?
>
> CLASS: (various responses) True, true, I feel you.
>
> JEREMY: Mister, I love this whole in-the-park thing, but may I go to the bathroom?
>
> TEACHER: What? I can't hear you, and why are you talking like that? You sound mad different. Jose, can you tell me why he's talking like that?

JOSE: I don't even know fam. Yo, Jeremy? Why are you talking mad funny? Like you sound like you in a school or something?

JEREMY: Oh wait, what? Oh, ya'll buggin'. Fine. Yo, mister, I need to go pee.

TEACHER: Aight bet. Go ahead.

For the length of time this exercise was going on, the whole class was expected to engage using only the local neoindigenous slang of the Washington Heights neighborhood of New York City, where they all came from. For ten minutes, this was the privileged language. After the session, the teacher could extend the exercise by switching to another context in which another language is privileged. In this case, the teacher restarted the exercise by having students imagine themselves walking through the freshly manicured lawn of an Ivy League college on their way to a meeting of distinguished scientists. Once they opened their eyes, they were in the meeting and had to converse with each other using the language and codes of this new setting. The student who had left the classroom to go to the bathroom in the scenario described above returned to find the class in a much different place than when he'd left.

JEREMY: (Hurriedly walking back to his seat from the door of the classroom) Ayo I'm back. What we talking 'bout now?

TEACHER: Pardon me, sir, but the class was in the midst of a discussion when you abruptly interrupted.

JOSE: While you were at the lavatory, we commenced a discussion about Newton's laws and their origin.

JEREMY: (Without missing a beat) My most sincere apologies, class, please proceed.

In this new exercise, the use of neoindigenous language is now frowned upon, as students who may never have been in a college setting before transition to the norms of these spaces without ever leaving the classroom. These exercises enable students to see how the various descriptions of photosynthesis ("The sun gets lyte and blings on the whole joint"; "The light shines on the whole leaf"; and "Photons are emitted on the surface area of the leaf") are each correct, but only in specific contexts. The teacher may work with students to further extend this exercise beyond language to dress and other forms of social interaction.

In the classroom, then, it is imperative that students' neoindigenous dialect and culture are respected. Their ways of dress, speech, and interaction must be valued. In this type of classroom, the teacher assesses content knowledge simply on the merit of its conceptual and scientific accuracy and not on the ways that the information is shared. This means that answers to questions can be in slang, and students can express themselves naturally.

In many cases, once educators reach the point where students are actively engaged and fully themselves in the classroom, they believe they have done the work necessary to improve education for their students; however, they've just begun. After students are fully engaged, the teacher begins to introduce youth to the discourse of power in its varied forms. The nature of, and need for, code switching should be discussed with the students, in addition to the reasons for the whole discourse approach and the imagination exercises. For example, students are shown that *light* and *lyte* have the same meaning, but in places where only traditional English is accepted, spelling the word as "lyte" would not be acceptable even though it makes more sense to use "lyte" and not "light." "Light," if pronounced as it is spelled, would be "lig-hit." They are told that if it is spelled as it sounds, the neoindigenous spelling would make more sense. The teacher must then share with students that spelling or saying the word in the way that "makes sense" would be marked wrong in certain contexts, and should be learned and mastered.

————

When neoindigenous youth are introduced to the concept of code switching, and have engaged in it deliberately and consistently in the classroom, they become proficient in strategically using it beyond the classroom in a way that is not disingenuous or inauthentic. When they can code switch with fluency, and appreciate why they do so, they enter new social spaces with a comfort and courage that taps into their cosmopolitan ethos. As they employ socially constructed codes and rules while maintaining their own cultural identities, they force the world to see past these same codes and rules when indentifying the brilliance of young people.

CHAPTER 11

Curation and Computing

Having been invited to be a fellow at the Hiphop Archive and Research Institute at Harvard University, I walked into a room that captured almost forty years of hip-hop culture through a variety of artifacts. There were pieces of art, articles of clothing, turntables, and books that faced modern flat-screen televisions. Each served as a powerful conversation starter, and together they made a cohesive presentation. What was most powerful about the space was how it served as an authentic and living learning environment. A class was being held at the institute, with students' work displayed on a television screen. These offerings fit in perfectly with the historical artifacts in the room. The students were co-curating the history of hip-hop in real time.

In *Liberating Culture*, a powerful book about the nature of museums and cultural heritage preservation, Christina Kreps describes her work within institutions that curate indigenous artifacts. She tells stories about the challenge of working as a museum curator to capture an indigenous culture that she was not part of, while being viewed in museums as a specialist because she was a Westerner with a certain type of expertise. In many ways her experience in museums reminded me of the experiences of white folks who teach in the hood. She had expertise in terms of academic knowledge and credentials, but was far from expert on the indigenous themselves. In her book, Kreps goes on to describe the fact that there is, and has always been, a cross-cultural phenomenon that embraces the preservation of artifacts that have cultural significance—especially among the indigenous. Within indigenous groups, artifacts have always been collected so that they can be interacted with, learned from, and celebrated. Kreps argues that returning the art of curation to the community (even within institutions of power like museums) changes the relationship between the community and the institution. By privileging the voice of the indigenous curator, individuals from the culture/community "bring to the museum a newly added dimension of human potential and experience" that those within the museums can learn and grow from.[1] In much the same way, the neoindigenous gain a powerful new platform when youth curate their everyday experiences in schools and offer their unique perspective on phenomena and experiences that would otherwise be lost. The chief work for the museum curator or the urban educator then becomes to create the context in which youth are able to curate their own lived experiences. Once these experiences are curated—identified, collected, packaged, shared—they become teaching tools for both the students and the teacher.

Toward a New Curation: The Power of Video

In reality pedagogy, working with youth to curate the school experience is a significant aspect of the pedagogical process. Here, the use of video is a way to enhance powerful practice and reflect on past performance.

My use of student-curated video began when I selected representatives from a class I taught to participate in a cogen. I invited them to meet me for lunch, and was excited to hear what plans of action we could cogenerate to improve the class. Once the students had assembled and taken their seats, I asked them what major issue was getting in the way of their learning. I grabbed my pen to take notes, and before long a powerful conversation was underway.

Within two minutes, they had all agreed that the biggest issue for each of them was that I was raising my voice too often or yelling at students when I got frustrated. Students mentioned that my yelling distracted them, made them upset, and put them in a mood that made them disinterested in learning. As they spoke, I felt my blood boil. How could they say that I yelled and got in the way of their learning when I obviously cared enough to have this very conversation? As they elaborated on my behavior in the classroom, my immediate reaction was to tell students to identify another issue that would not target me directly. However, it was much easier for me to just end the meeting. Somehow, it seemed like they were just being vindictive and were attacking me without merit. I announced that the cogen was over and that we would try it another time when they were willing to take it more seriously. The students seemed confused, but didn't seem too concerned that I ended the meeting. They each walked out of the room, and everything returned to normal when I saw them in the classroom the next day.

The next week, I invited the same students to participate in another cogen. They begrudgingly walked in, and I once again suggested that they share their suggestions for improving the classroom. Again, students unanimously suggested that we should all address the negative atmosphere that resulted from my yelling at them. Once again, I was unprepared for hearing the truth and ended the dialogue prematurely. As I closed the meeting, I reiterated to the students that I wanted them to take the cogens seriously and identify real issues that were impeding their learning. Without explicitly saying it, I was telling students that I didn't believe their issue with my yelling was a genuine one. A third meeting was scheduled for the following week.

On this final cogen, as I greeted the participants and explained the rules of the dialogue once again, one student brought up the issue of my teaching style. However, this time she chose to make the point by presenting a video montage of my class from the previous two weeks, which indeed documented me yelling at students. Because I had denied that my yelling at students was an issue, she had used her smartphone to record my class and then spliced together clips showing me yelling at the class.

At this point, although it was still tough to accept, I realized that if four students who represented different groups in the classroom were agreeing that this was an issue, it was something that I needed to address. As soon as I acknowledged my behavior as a problem, the students began to work with me to fix it. Quickly, one student suggested that whenever I was raising my voice to a level that was uncomfortable for students, the four students in the cogen group would let me know by lightly tapping on their desks and making eye contact with me to alert me to the situation. In turn, whenever I had the inclination to yell but caught myself addressing the issue, I would also tap on my desk and give the four students eye contact. We would then respond to each other by nodding in agreement to acknowledge the moment and what was happening.

During the next class, as students filed into the classroom and found their seats, I went through my regular routine of asking them to put their homework from the night before on the table so that I could collect it. I walked through the rows in the classroom, picked up the students' assignments, and then got to a student who did not have anything on her desk. Before I knew it, I was raising my voice in frustration because she had missed yet another assignment. As my voice began to rise, I heard a tapping sound from four different places in the room. It took a second or two for me to realize what was going on, but then I looked up and met the gazes of the students from the cogen group. I immediately realized that I was being called out for raising my voice. My cogen students were implementing the plan of action we had cogenerated. In response, I took a step back, breathed in deeply and deliberately, and lowered my voice to ask the student why she didn't have her assignment. She looked up at me, told me that she didn't understand the assignment, and showed me a piece of paper that showed her attempts at the task. As she explained her difficulty, I looked up to see four smiles from different parts of the room that indicated that a breakthrough of sorts had occurred. And from that moment on, the entire class seemed to run better.

The identification of an issue, and the capturing and preserving of that issue on tape, created an opportunity for me to be more reflective about my practice. That experience led to my belief that part of the work of teaching well is allowing youth to critique their learning environments.

Video is a powerful tool in all aspects of reality pedagogy, allowing students to harness technology to validate their experiences both within the classroom and in their own communities. It can be used for the purposes of coteaching and as a way to capture cosmopolitanism in action. When students are charged with preserving, capturing, and then sharing their experiences in the school and in the community, teaching and learning becomes dialogic—with students and their curated artifacts providing conversation pieces and inspiration for reflection, much like the best museum installations.

Neoindigenous Communities and Social Media

One of the most powerful types of ethnography and arenas for curation in the contemporary world exists on social media. Cyber ethnography and digital curation provides information for educators that they would otherwise not be privy to, and that is necessary for studying given the communal ways of knowing and being of the neoindigenous, and the fact that white folks who teach in the hood have little to no access to these worlds. Consequently, I argue that one of the most powerful ways for the educator to gain insight into the world of the neoindigenous is to develop an understanding of the online communities of which they are a part.

I came to an understanding of the significance of this work a few years ago, as I walked excitedly into a school I worked in that had just received a grant to buy its first class set of laptop computers. Previously, this school had been one of the last to receive up-to-date technology and Internet access in the city. The grant came after a plethora of academic articles, news reports, and internal documents by the Department of Education described a digital divide between the rich and poor across the city. These documents revealed how communities like the one I was working in were suffering the most as a result of not having access to technology and the Internet. The entire building was filled with excitement about the prospect of students finally being able to use computers, gaining access to the same technology their peers in other schools were receiving.

For the educators, getting computers meant that we would be able to better prepare students for college and careers in the real world. I was particularly excited, being the person on staff who was charged with teaching about and with the new computers. About three weeks after the laptops arrived at the school, and after badgering the school administrator to give me access to them, I was given the keys to a storage room in the basement where the laptops had been stored. After retrieving the laptops, I asked the administrator in charge about what plans, if any, were in place for the computers. She told me that they were to be exclusively used for enrichment through the math skills game that came with the order. Each day for the next week, I responded as I was instructed. As the students walked in, I assigned them to a laptop, loaded up the math game, and had students play the game. Initially this was exciting for the students because they had never used the laptops in school before. They were intrigued by the novelty of the computer, learning the game, and in theory, learning math as they played. This lasted for about a week until the students figured out how to beat the game (which was only a trial version) and quickly grew bored by what they saw as just another form of classroom busy work.

Students soon began asking me about access to the Internet and most importantly, how they could use the computers to actually enhance what they were learning in the classroom. I had no immediate answer to their questions and could only tell them what I had been told—which was that the laptops were to be used for the math game only. In response, students became increasingly frustrated whenever I carted the laptops into the room. What was intended to be an amazing teaching tool had become something that the students deeply resented.

When I discussed this with the school administrator, she recommended that I teach students how to type on the laptops in addition to playing the math game. Her specific suggestion was that I give the students excerpts from the textbook to type as a classroom activity. In compliance with my administrator's request, I assigned this task to my students when I returned to the classroom. Before long, students had grown even more frustrated than they were before. Eventually, they began to express this frustration by purposefully damaging the laptops by removing the keyboard keys. Once the school administration found out what students were doing to the computers, they were upset, and I was reprimanded for allowing the students to vandalize the computers.

Once word got out about the damage students had done to some of the laptops, faculty began to gripe about how "destructive and unappreciative those kids are." The white folks who teach in the hood seemed almost gleeful that their preconceptions about these urban students had been validated. It seemed like no one on the faculty was able to make the connection between the "destructive behavior" of the students and the inability of the school (myself included) to use the technology in ways that truly engaged and educated the students. The students were sending the adults in the school a message, the adults were not able to read the messages they were sending us, and before long, the principal ordered that the laptops be removed from the classroom and returned to the storage room in the school's basement.

About a month later, the school had become wired for the Internet for a few weeks, and the entire school was wondering whether or not it was sensible to put the laptops back in the hands of students. The damaged laptops had been repaired, and even though they were purchased for the students' use, the general consensus was that they should be kept away from them. Over time, the students forgot about the laptops, and the faculty seemed to as well. They remained in the storage closet in the school basement for weeks. Somehow, the initial enthusiasm in the beginning of the year surrounding giving youth access to technology and working toward equity had been replaced by maintaining the status quo.

Given my role as the teacher in charge of technology, I felt guilty for the current state of affairs. Perhaps if I hadn't reported the damage to the laptops, they wouldn't have been taken away. I also struggled to find out how I could convince the rest of the faculty that the students picked the keys off the laptops for a reason. They were not being destructive because of an inherent desire to do so, but because of their frustration. After a few unsuccessful attempts to convince the administration and my colleagues that it was worthwhile to allow students to have access to the technology again, I decided that I had no choice but to give the students access to the laptops despite being told that I should not. I knew that if students were actually being academically challenged when using the laptops, they would respect the devices and use them as they were intended to be used. We had not had access to the Internet prior to the laptops being taken away and with access to the Internet now, I was convinced that I could push the boundaries of what classroom learning was like and be more creative with the use of the laptops.

One afternoon after school, after staying late to work on lesson plans, I retrieved the computers from the storage room and carted them back into my classroom. I checked each one to ensure that they had access to the Internet, stored them in the closet closest to my desk, and left for the day. At home that night, I decided that I was going to design lessons around use of the laptops that would be imaginative and creative, knowing that it was the rote math games that drove the students to being destructive in the beginning of the year, and decided to identify websites that had new information and resources for students. After much thought, I decided to design a digital scavenger hunt related to the content I was teaching. The activity for the students would involve youth surfing the Web to discover websites that related to the classroom content. After planning and identifying all that could possibly go wrong, I decided that students would use the laptops during my next class. Surfing the Web would be a new activity for many of them and exploring these websites would be new and exciting.

The lesson incorporated a powerful driving question, a quick as-signment for students to complete, and a short lecture; the students were engaged. I then began distributing laptops to complete the final phase of my lesson. As I handed out the laptops, there was a look of disappointment across the faces of the students. They were enjoying the lesson thus far, and seeing the laptops brought back memories of being forced to sit and play a math game. This runs counter to just about all the research on using technology and the unbridled en-thusiasm that is supposed to come with using laptops in classrooms. Their responses to being handed the laptops once again showed that for the neoindigenous, the traditional rules do not apply. The technology alone was not enough to engage them. What they cared about was how it was being used. With this in mind, I pushed forward with my lesson and mentioned that we would be surfing the Inter-net and gathering information about our lesson from the computer. They weren't quite sure what I meant, but seemed relieved that they weren't being asked to play the math game.

Students responded by delving deeply into the assignment. They scoured through the list of websites I gave them, and began looking for the facts I asked them to. Before long, they were discussing with each other across the classroom about websites they had found and the facts they were uncovering. Rather than have them practice typ-ing or copying a passage from their textbooks, I asked them to record any new sites/information they were discovering and then share this information with their peers. A collective enthusiasm filled the room for the entire class period, until students tried to access websites that I had asked them to visit but that had been blocked by the school. I had identified the websites at home, with unrestricted Internet access. However, accessing the Internet at school meant that the students had a number of filters that wouldn't allow them full access to the Web, and in some cases no access to the sites I asked them to visit.

Once again, students began expressing the same frustrations they had experienced previously with the laptops. Students mentioned that the computers were broken and that the websites I asked them to visit didn't work. They couldn't finish the assignment I gave them, and that made them upset because they were actually enjoying the process of visiting websites and reading/learning new information. I didn't want their frustration to lead to them purposefully damaging the laptops again, and so I stood in front of the class at a crossroads. I didn't want to be like every other adult in the school who didn't believe in them, but I also didn't want to risk the possibility of them taking their frustrations out on the laptops.

As I stood in front of the class trying to figure out what my next steps would be, a pair of students at the back of the classroom who were still engaged with their laptops began to giggle and give each other high fives. Curious, I walked to the back of the class to see what was up. When I got there, I discovered that the students had found a way to use a proxy server to access the websites that the rest of the class didn't have access to. A proxy server is an indirect connection to the Internet through an outside source that has a different (outside) IP address and not the network or the local Internet connection. This was the first time many of these students were able to use the Internet, and I was shocked that they even knew what a proxy server was. Just a few minutes before, I had been showing students how to type websites into the search bar, and now these two students had found a way to overcome a major technological challenge and complete their assignment.

The news of the students' discovery spread like wildfire across the classroom. Before long everyone was on the Internet visiting websites that had previously been blocked, allowing them to complete their assignment. The next day, they asked for the laptops almost as soon as they walked into the classroom. Again, they completed their assignments, and then, very quickly, began to sign on to, and start communicating via, social media. This was over a decade ago, before the more popular websites like Facebook and Twitter had gained traction. However, students quickly found sites like MySpace, Sconex, and other chat rooms in which to communicate. What was most interesting to me at the time was how quickly they gravitated toward social media. For the students, getting on social media was intuitive. They learned how to navigate these sites quickly and develop networks with each other and other neoindigenous youth from other geographic settings. Within months, accessing the laptops for social media was the primary activity of just about every student in that class and beyond it.

Many students didn't have access to computers at home, and so they would get passes to come to my class during lunch or after school to use the laptops. Students who didn't have me as a teacher would schedule appointments to use the computers in my classroom, and would wait patiently for hours after school so that they could create accounts and use social media. The power of these sites led me to begin exploring their potential for use in neoindigenous classrooms. In response, I ensured that they used these platforms to share homework assignments with each other, plan school activities, and even create profiles dedicated to topics I was teaching. On the course to further exploring the possibilities of using social media as a teaching tool, I came to recognize the significance of technology to the neoindigenous. These populations are the early adopters of a number of major technological breakthroughs and social media platforms because of the way the technology aligns to their forms of cultural exchange. Just as hip-hop culture pushed the norms of music production technology and shaped the ways that microphones, speakers, and turntables were designed and used, the neoindigenous have done the same thing with social media.

For example, a website like Twitter allows for rapid-fire exchanges within neoindigenous communities that affect their lives in some way. Consequently, constellations of the neoindigenous converge onto Twitter daily and utilize it as a space for venting frustrations or reacting to phenomena in a way that is a technological version of what they already do in real life. Communities like black Twitter (a nonexclusive gathering of people of color who converge on Twitter when major events that affect the black community emerge) provide powerful examples of how this happens. Younger people within this group are oftentimes middle and high school students and use sites like Twitter and Facebook in much the same way that my middle school students used MySpace and Sconex.

The interesting thing about social media as it relates to education is that the pairing has the potential to positively transform education, but this hasn't been explored deeply because of a fear of social media by educators and school administrators. Most schools across the country have a ban on social media use in schools, and prohibit teachers from exchanging with students via social media outside of school. The underlying premise is the false belief that there is no useful connection between social media and schools and that teachers and students should not be engaging in conversations outside schools that may lead to inappropriate exchanges. As a school administrator once told me, "There was no social media when I went to school and I received a good education. There is no reason why students need that now." Unfortunately, what has occurred as a result of excluding social media from schools is that students then infer that these platforms are completely unrelated to learning. Consequently, they engage in social media solely for the purpose of social interaction, which in turn validates educators' reasons for banning it from school.

Reality pedagogues avoid this cycle that maintains the dysfunctional use of a potentially powerful pedagogical tool and instead focus on using social media as a space for learning. This process includes creating a classroom Facebook page that highlights the class name, homework assignments, members of the class, books they are reading, and links to YouTube videos that relate to classroom content. On the Facebook page, students can converse about classwork, and begin to blur the lines between in-school and out-of-school activities. The class can also have a Twitter page where professionals in the field the course is focused on become part of the social network of the class. Of course, when introducing social media in the classroom, it's crucial to first instruct students in and set guidelines for its appropriate use.

In research done on and with youth from more affluent socioeconomic backgrounds, it is widely accepted that "engaging in various forms of social media is a routine activity that benefits children and adolescents by enhancing communication, social connection, and even technical skills."[2] However, when it comes to the neoindigenous, there is a stigma associated with the use of social media in the creation of underground communities. Consider, for example, websites like the wildly popular and deeply problematic WorldStarHipHop, which was developed by a young man from Queens, New York, as an alternate news/information/media site for young people from communities similar to his. The site was created as a place where audiences can respond to video, but many of the expressions take a deeply negative turn as urban youth find an outlet to stake their claims. This in turn validates those who believe social media is inimical to learning.

Allowing social media to have a more positive impact on the neoindigenous requires teaching about, and using these tools, in their schools. It also requires studying the ways they engage with these tools productively, and then celebrating these forms of engagement. Most importantly, it requires working with youth toward using these tools productively. For example, despite knowing how easily accessible social media is, the neoindigenous do not make (or care to make) connections between its accessibility/utility and scrutiny by colleges, jobs, and the general public. This means that those who are ignorant of the nuances and subtleties of neoindigenous culture may read students' digital footprints (track their social media and Web presence) and draw inaccurate conclusions about who they are. Creating an online presence is a skill that should be taught in classrooms. Furthermore, many of the neoindigenous are unaware of how to use their social media presence to extend and build upon social networks that may include professionals in their fields of interest or future careers. The reality pedagogue understands these realities, and ensures that youth gain opportunities to maximize their life opportunities while directly assessing, learning, and using the tools that have significance in/on their lives.

#HipHopEd & Tweeting: Digital Ethnography

One of the most popular and intuitive social media platforms is Twitter. This microblogging platform allows participants to share thoughts, ideas, and commentary on a wide array of topics to others who engage with them on the site. In my work, I have used Twitter to engage audiences who are interested in the intersections of hip-hop and education through the hashtag #HipHopEd. A hashtag is a topic or theme placed right after the # symbol that people who tweet add to their messages in order to indicate the broader topic that they are talking about. #HipHopEd is one of these hashtags, and has grown to become a worldwide conversation that takes place every Tuesday at 9:00 p.m. EST.

During this weekly chat, educators from across the globe converge on Twitter and exchange lesson plans, resources, recommendations for music, thoughts, and opinions. The conversations grow quickly, are wide ranging under the larger umbrella of hip-hop and education, and have a distinct neoindigenous tenor. By this I mean that the virtual conversations on Twitter take on the structure of a black barbershop conversation in relation to the overlapping exchanges, quick responses, and general emotional tone. Over the last four years that I have facilitated this social media conversation, I have been able to chart the participation of a number of regular commentators, and measure their increased engagement in dialogues and growth as teachers and students. In efforts to replicate the successful dialogues that happen during #HipHopEd, I have worked with many educators across middle school, high school, and college classes to engage their students using Twitter. In these classrooms, students sign on to the Twitter website at the beginning of the semester or academic year, create an account, and then tweet during the class using a pre-established hashtag. In each of these classes, students chose to engage in powerful dialogues during the class, and also after the classes were over.

Unfortunately, in some schools, access to sites like Twitter are blocked, and the opportunity to engage students using powerful digital tools is lost. In response, I have experimented with using paper versions of digital platforms. Paper-based versions of Twitter are powerful ways to engage youth in the classroom, allowing them to move around the class, listen attentively, engage with their peers, and learn content during lectures by the teacher. The process includes having students create a handle, creating a Twitter board in the class, sharing the rules for the tweeting process, identifying the classroom hashtag, and getting the class to participate.

The creating a name/handle process begins in much the same way that one would sign on to the website. Students are asked to pick a username based on a nickname or some variation of the student's real name that they want to be called in class. Students will then be asked to write their username on a sheet of construction paper, fold the sheet so their name is visible to anyone looking at it, and then place it on their desk. For many among the neoindigenous, allowing them to bring their Internet handles or out-of-school nicknames into the classroom allows them to bring parts of their identity that are usually silenced in the classroom to the fore. While the teacher may elect not to call students by these names during the regular class, when they are engaged in "classroom Twitter," it should be permitted, and students should be encouraged to communicate with each other using those handles as well. Engaging in this process, and this step in particular, allows the teacher to bring one of the most appealing parts of Twitter to the classroom; the creation of an online persona through a Twitter handle/name.

The next step in the process is for the teacher to post a large sheet of paper on a visible surface in the class. This board or sheet of paper serves as the equivalent of a Twitter timeline. It is the place where the classroom communication is captured and where exchanges around a topic begin, develop, and then get captured for future use or reference. The Twitter board or sheet always begins with a "tweet" sent by the teacher to one of the students in the classroom, about what is currently being discussed in class. Once one has been created, teachers may use it as a teaching resource during future lectures, or a way to review topics already covered in the classroom.

The final step is to explain the Twitter classroom process. This involves the teacher letting the students know that the teacher sends/writes the first tweet. When someone has been tweeted, they have to come up to the front of the class (or wherever the Twitter board has been placed) and respond. A person cannot be tweeted more than five times during a class. Everyone must be prepared to answer the question that was tweeted to them, and then tweet a question to someone else, and if someone does not have an answer to a question that was tweeted to them, they may ask a question to someone else. The main hashtag (which will be written by the teacher and would be the main theme of the lecture) can only be shifted to include something else that has been discussed during the class. The students "tweet" by writing their responses at the Twitter board with a marker that the teacher makes available to them, and once they begin engaging in the process, it doesn't end until the teacher writes a closing tweet.

An example of a classroom Twitter exchange among four students and the teacher that took place as the teacher was teaching the topic of energy is provided below. Previous to the teacher sending the first tweet, the students had displayed their Twitter names on their desks, and the class had done a few activities related to the topic.

> @BXFLYEST: What are the two types of #energy? [Sent by the teacher to open the exchange]
>
> @BXFLYEST: Potential and Kinetic #energy? @CoolCarlos What is another way to describe Potential #Energy? [Sent from a student to another based on information the teacher just shared while lecturing]
>
> @COOLCARLOS: Potential energy is also called stored energy. #Energy before it is in action. @JRealz What is a way to describe kinetic energy?
>
> @JREALZ: Kinetic is energy in motion. #Energy when it is released. @JessicaF What is the #formula for finding Kinetic energy?
>
> @JESSICAF: KE = ½ m(v*v) @JRealz What about the #formula for Potential Energy?

The use of classroom Twitter is an activity that looks very different from what we see in a traditional classroom. It requires that students are able to stand up during the teacher's lecture and that they are engaged in a way that allows for their multimodal neoindigenous nature to be expressed in the classroom. The activity pushes them to pay close attention to the teacher, the Twitter board, and each other in a way that allows them to bring their full selves to the classroom.

Another activity that brings social media into the classroom is the use of "classroom Instagram." This process brings the powerful visual and communication aspects of Instagram to the classroom in a way that allows youth to exchange with each other and use images related to the content to drive their exchanges. This process involves the creation of a template that looks like the homepage of the popular social media site, and the same process of creating a name/handle as was described with classroom Twitter. The process of creating a homepage simply involves using a large sheet of paper, painting a border around it, and drawing a box near the top of the page where an image will be placed. This activity can also include having students design the template themselves so that the teacher can simply use their page template for the activity.

Once a template has been created, an image is placed on it for students to respond to. For example, in a science class, the teacher may place an image or other artistic representation of a phenomenon being described, and then students would respond to it based on what they may have learned or read. This activity works particularly well when the image that the teacher presents is of a historical figure and the students in the class are assigned to roles of others in that person's life. One way that I have seen this activity used is when the teacher assigned a number of students to be historical figures with Instagram accounts, and then gave the students the assignment to find images of the person they were assigned on the Internet, and then post pictures to the classroom Instagram and allow other students to comment on it. In one particularly compelling example of this activity, a student was tweeting as Martin Luther King Jr. and created a timeline of sorts of his life through popular images using contemporary language. In one picture with Coretta Scott King, he placed the caption, "She always got my back #rideordie." This use of historical images, with contemporary language in an Instagram template, blurs the lines between the historical and the contemporary and draws students into the content being taught in powerful ways. Most importantly, it provides the educator with a powerful set of curated archives from the classroom for future use in the classroom.

Metalogues

Metalogues merge the types of exchanges that occur on social media with student-curated artifacts, creating a powerful classroom norm that students respond positively to and that allows the teacher to gain keen insight into important aspects of what is happening in the classroom. Gregory Bateson conducted the first metalogue for a purpose that is far from teaching and learning, but its structure has proven to be very effective as a way to generate reflection in classrooms. In Bateson's iteration of the metalogue, and other academic work related to the practice, the goal is to create a "written dialogue" that enhances metacognitive abilities through a natural process of exchange.[3]

In the classroom, metalogues are a way for students and their teacher to engage in conversations about the classroom in a way that takes on the same structure as the cogenerative dialogue, but involves written exchanges between the teacher and the student. The metalogue also varies from the cogen in that it can occur among all students within a selected peer group during the classroom and focuses on informal assessments of learning in conjunction with addressing the students' feelings about the teacher, the classroom context, and the instruction.

The metalogue begins with the teacher/school purchasing notebooks for groups of students that will remain in the classroom for the rest of the academic year. Each metalogue group consists of four students that the teacher selects to work together for the course of the academic year. These four students will share a notebook, and will communicate with each other through this notebook when they are in class. The students who will be in the metalogue groups can be selected using the same process that the teacher uses to select cogen participants (in that they should represent different types of students in the classroom), and do not necessarily have to be sitting together or have relationships with each other during regular class time.

When the teacher calls for a metalogue, one of the students in each group goes to a designated place in the classroom where the notebooks are held, and returns to a seat close to members of his or her group (students can self-manage the seating arrangements during this process). Once all the students are seated, the teacher then poses the metalogue question of the day, which can range from a question about the content that is being taught, a review of the lesson or day, or a general description of the class and how students feel it is going. During the metalogue, students will be engaging in a process that seems a lot like passing notes in class. One student begins responding to the teacher's question in the book, and then passes the notebook to another member of the group to respond to the question or continue the train of thought of the first student who starts writing. This process continues until all students have passed the notebook to each other, and have each written in the book for a few "rounds." Rounds here refer to the number of cycles that the notebook has been passed to each member of the group, and for a complete metalogue to happen at least one round must be completed. The nature of the writing depends greatly on the type of question, or the prompt given. For example, if the teacher asks a typical metalogue question like "What did we do in class today?" The metalogue response takes on a narrative form, as illustrated by two excerpts from youth metalogues below:

PROMPT: What did we do in class today?

JANET: First we walked in the classroom, and we were asked to go to a lab table and pick up materials like . . .

SHAWN: . . . popsicle sticks, pipe cleaners, index cards, and paper clips. We then returned to our seats and . . .

JOSE A: . . . were given handouts with instructions on creating a model of DNA. We were told not to start playing with the materials yet but . . .

DYWANA: . . . a lot of students started early and began to play with the materials. Our group listened attentively though and we . . .

Another metalogue students created had the following prompt: "Construct a story using the vocabulary words we learned in class today." This was a more cerebral activity where students used vocabulary words to co-construct a story.

PROMPT: Write a story using the vocabulary words *disintegration, assimilation, emphasize, degenerate, limitation, rehashing,* and *audacity.*

JOSE: In a conversation between two friends who had an argument about another friend they no longer speak to, the friends began rehashing their past experiences together . . .

JANET: The conversation quickly started focusing on the disintegration of their friendship and what could be done to . . .

SHAWN: . . . avoid the degenerate they were once friends with who stole . . . money from them both and then had the audacity to . . .

In the examples above, one student writes down the prompt, and begins writing while the other members of the group try to think about what the person is writing, and the possible responses to what is being written. Together, all members of the group co-construct the response to the teacher's prompt. The baton exchanges between the students are separated by using the ellipsis as a symbol of a shift in authorship from one person to another, and they all learn how to engage in a task together. During these metalogues, one successful practice has been assigning a pen color (red, black, blue, green) to each member of the group. The purpose of using different color pens is so that the teacher can follow the responses of a specific group of students over the course of the academic year. For example, if students are grouped based on academic ability, skill level, or even the class they were in during the previous year, giving these students a specific color to write with can help the teacher to easily chart/assess how particular students are doing by picking up a few metalogue notebooks and reading the comments written by students in a specific color.

When conducting the metalogue, it is important to set the appropriate classroom environment. One successful practice is playing instrumentals from popular songs that the students listen to in the background every time that the teacher proposes the activity. I have had students write the name of a song they want to hear in class on an index card and place the name of the song in a bag that sits on my desk. During the metalogue or other activities that require the students to write or work without much interaction with the teacher, I select a song from the bag to play during the activity. The music sets the context for the task that students are about to engage in, and allows them to think of the activity as a release from the structure of the traditional class. In many ways the structure of the metalogue is similar to the popular DEAR (Drop Everything and Read) program that is implemented in many urban schools as a way to encourage youth to read. During DEAR, the school announces that everyone will begin reading, and the entire student body grabs a book from the classroom library or reaches for one they are already reading, and begins to read. During this program, there is usually complete silence in the class or in the school, and students literally drop everything to read. The notion of carving out the space to stop what they're doing and read—even in the middle of a lesson—is powerful and announces to students that reading is valued within the school, and that it is an important activity. This is the type of feeling that students experience when engaged in the metalogue. The difference between DEAR and the metalogue is rooted in the recognition of the reality pedagogue that for many neoindigenous youth whose everyday lives involve the creation of, and embeddedness in music/ noise/sound, the requirement of complete silence in schools creates tremendous symbolic violence. Students stop what they're doing to engage in the metalogue, but participating in the process is framed as something that they not only benefit from, but enjoy doing.

The final and perhaps most valuable aspect of the metalogue is the way in which it enables the teacher to communicate with students and assess their learning without waiting for standardized exams or tests. The teacher can always pick up a few metalogue notebooks to read and respond to after school or on a weekend. This is not a task like grading tests that is time-sensitive and oftentimes overwhelming. The teacher reviews, writes comments and responses to metalogues, and identifies students that may or may not be engaging in the class through their responses to their peers. At whatever point the teacher has written feedback to all metalogue groups, one of the metalogue prompts can be a group response to the teacher's comments.

Oftentimes I hear the question, What are students supposed to be doing when one person in their group is writing? My response is always that they are thinking, reflecting, and listening to the music playing in the background so that when the notebook comes back to them, they are ready to write.

———

The larger philosophies and teacher practices outlined in this chapter describe some contemporary approaches to implementing reality pedagogy. They support the larger work of preparing teachers to become students of their neoindigenous students, both through the students themselves and the artifacts they produce.

CONCLUSION

Completion
Thoughts on Transformative Teaching

Throughout this work, I have provided educators and those interested in the field of education a number of concepts to think about, new approaches to consider, and new practices to implement. However, in my work as a teacher and a trainer of teachers, there are times when the work seems too tough, inspiration is nowhere to be found, and I am so bogged down by attacks on the profession and shifting policies that lead nowhere that I must take a step back and regroup. In this final chapter, I share some thoughts I always return to on my journey in education. They are a collection of personal musings, shared with the sole intent of supporting educators on their most challenging days and reminding them of why we do this work, and what we need to do it well.

———

The way that a teacher teaches can be traced directly back to the way that the teacher has been taught. The time will always come when teachers must ask themselves if they will follow the mold or blaze a new trail. There are serious risks that come with this decision. It essentially boils down to whether one chooses to do damage to the system or to the student.

———

The longer teachers teach, the better they are at their practice. That practice may serve to empower students or it may break the students' spirit. That decision belongs to the teacher.

———

The effectiveness of the teacher can be traced directly back to what that teacher thinks of the student. If the teacher does not value the student, there is no motivation to take risks to engage with the student. It is easier and safer to remain in the traditional model—even though that model has failed the student.

———

How successful the teacher is in the classroom is directly related to how successful the teacher thinks the students can be. Teachers limit themselves and their students when they put caps on what their students can achieve.

———

Teachers who hold within themselves perceptions of the inadequacy of students will never be able to teach them to be something greater than what they are. You cannot teach someone you do not believe in.

———

Planning for your lesson is valuable, but being willing to let go of that plan is even more so. It is only on the path away from where you started that you can get to where you want to go.

———

Continued effort in teaching more effectively inevitably results in more effective teaching. However, this all depends on what the teacher considers to be effective. The teacher must ask what the desired result of the teaching is. You cannot be effective if you have not defined for yourself what *effective* means.

———

The kind of teacher you will become is directly related to the kind of teachers you associate with. Teaching is a profession where misery does more than just love company—it recruits, seduces, and romances it. Avoid people who are unhappy and disgruntled about the possibilities for transforming education. They are the enemy of the spirit of the teacher.

A Note from
the Series Editor

As I was reading this book, I remembered Dr. Emdin's March 2014 Simmons College—Beacon Press Race, Education, and Democracy Lectures, upon which this book is based. To the rapt audience, overflowing with high school and college students, teachers and teacher educators, community activists and organizers, the excitement was palpable. The young and the elderly enthusiastically embraced Dr. Emdin's ideas about urban education and urban youth. Most importantly, all of us in the room could feel Dr. Emdin's passion, love, and respect for our youth.

Dr. Emdin has brought his considerable passion and expertise to this outstanding and important book. It comes at a time when we are overwhelmed by descriptions of urban students that have little resemblance to who they are. Situating himself as narrator, teacher, and teacher educator, Dr. Emdin makes visible the dominant narrative about teaching in urban schools, which ultimately debases what it means to be a teacher—"stories about angry and violent urban youth who [do] not want to be in school and [do] not want to learn."

Dr. Emdin forces us to pay attention to an unquestioned assertion that is routinely and glibly communicated in school reform circles: "urban students have to be saved from their communities." Instead of the community being a place for students to be saved from, Dr. Emdin conceptualizes the community as a location where teachers can experience and learn about community-based models of effective teaching and learning. He brilliantly and exquisitely describes and deconstructs the pedagogy and participant structures of the Pentecostal sermon, the barbershop and beauty shop, and the hip-hop cypher—formal and informal community-based cultural/institutional formations. He demonstrates how these models can be used to influence and improve the pedagogical practices of urban teachers.

Describing and theorizing urban youth as *neoindigenous*, Dr. Emdin situates students as members of a historically oppressed group, who are routinely educated for compliance. Here, also, Emdin offers us a powerful set of alternative practices and structures, under the descriptor *reality pedagogy*. He challenges us to meet "each student on his or her own cultural and emotional turf." Instead of being educated for compliance, the student is positioned as "the expert in his or her own teaching and learning," co-constructing the classroom with the teacher.

This book is filled with wisdom, theoretical and practical knowledge that has been formed in praxis. It is required reading for teachers, teacher educators, and community activists. Dr. Emdin brings the culture, insights, and genius of the hip-hop generation to the critical task of educating our youth for freedom.

This is an important book. It is smart, compelling, filled with emotions, and brimming over with commitment.

—Theresa Perry
Series Director
Professor of Africana Studies and Education
Simmons College
Boston, Massachusetts

Notes

Introduction

1. Robert Hays, *Editorializing "The Indian Problem": The New York Times on Native Americans, 1860–1900* (Carbondale: Southern Illinois University Press, 2007).

2. BIA Schools, Records of the Bureau of Indian Affairs, Record Group 75, National Archives and Records Administration, Washington, DC.

3. Benedict Anderson, *Imagined Communities: Reflections on the Origin and Spread of Nationalism* (London: Verso, 1983).

4. J. Park, "Ethnogenesis or Neoindigenous Intelligentsia: Contemporary Mapuche-Huilliche Poetry," *Latin American Research Review* 42, no. 3 (2007): 15–42.

5. Glen S. Aikenhead and Masakata Ogawa, "Indigenous Knowledge and Science Revisited," *Cultural Studies of Science Education* 2 (2007): 539–620.

6. Jason A. Okonofua and Jennifer L. Eberhardt, "Two Strikes: Race and the Disciplining of Young Students," *Psychological Science* 26 (2015): 617–24.

7. Gloria Ladson-Billings, "Toward a Theory of Culturally Relevant Pedagogy," *American Educational Research Journal* 32, no. 3 (Autumn 1995): 465–91.

8. Kathryn Davis and Rosemary Henze, "Applying Ethnographic Perspectives to Issues in Cross Cultural Pragmatics," *Journal of Pragmatics* 30 (1998): 399–419.

9. Manuhuia Barcham, "(De)Constructing the Politics of Indigeneity," in *Political Theory and the Rights of Indigenous Peoples*, ed. Duncan Ivison, Paul Patton, and Will Sanders (New York: Cambridge University Press, 2000), 137–51.

10. George J. Sefa Dei and Alireza Asgharzadeh, "Indigenous Knowledges and Globalization: An African Perspective," in *African Education and Globalization: Critical Perspectives*, ed. Ali A. Abdi, Korbla P. Puplampu, and George J. Sefa Dei (Lanham, MD: Lexington, 2006), 53–78.

11. M. Battiste, "Indigenous Knowledge: Foundations for First Nations," *World Indigenous Nations Higher Education Consortium (WINHEC) Journal*, 2005; Michel S. Laguerre, *Minoritized Space: An Inquiry into the Spatial Order of Things* (Berkeley, CA: Institute of Governmental Studies Press/ Institute of Urban and Regional Development, 1999).

12. Valentina Klenowski, "Assessment for Learning Revisited: An Asia-Pacific Perspective," *Assessment in Education: Principles, Policy & Practice* 16, no. 3 (2009): 277–82; K. Storry, "What Is Working in Good Schools in Remote Indigenous Communities?," *Issue Analysis* 86 (2007); Wharehuia Hemara, *Maori Pedagogies: A View from the Literature* (Wellington, NZ: New Zealand Council for Educational Research, 2000).

13. Langston Hughes, *The Ways of White Folks* (New York: Knopf, 1934).

Chapter 1: Camaraderie

1. Adrienne Rich, *Blood, Bread, and Poetry: Selected Prose, 1979–1985* (New York: Norton, 1986).

2. Kelly Oliver, *The Colonization of Psychic Space: A Psychoanalytic Social Theory of Oppression* (Minneapolis: University of Minnesota Press, 2004).

3. Ralph Ellison, *Invisible Man* (New York: Random House, 1952), 1.

4. John R. Searle, *The Construction of Social Reality* (New York: Free Press, 1995), 15.

5. See Eduardo Duran, *Healing the Soul Wound: Counseling with American Indians and Other Native Peoples* (New York: Teachers College Press, 2006); Mark Findlay, *The Globalisation of Crime: Understanding Transitional Relationships in Context* (Cambridge, UK: Cambridge University Press, 1999).

Chapter 2: Courage

1. See, inter alia, John Ogbu, *Black American Students in an Affluent Suburb: A Study of Academic Disengagement* (Mahwah, NJ: Erlbaum, 2003).

Chapter 4: Cogenerative Dialogues

1. Paulo Freire, *Pedagogy of the Oppressed* (New York: Continuum, 1982).

2. Kenneth George Tobin and Wolff-Michael Roth, *Teaching to Learn: A View from the Field* (Rotterdam: Sense, 2006); Christopher Emdin and E. Lehner, "Situating Cogenerative Dialogue in a Cosmopolitan Ethic," *Forum: Qualitative Social Research/Sozialforschung* 7, no. 2 (March 2006), http://www .qualitative-research.net/index.php/fqs/article/view/125.

3. George J. Gmelch, "Baseball Magic," *Trans-Action* 8, no. 8 (1971): 39–41, 54.

Chapter 5: Coteaching

1. Michael Cole, "What's Culture Got to Do with It? Education Research as a Necessarily Interdisciplinary Enterprise," *Educational Researcher* 39, no. 6 (2010): 461–70.

2. C. E. Finn, A. J. Rotherham, and C. R. Hokanson, eds., *Rethinking Special Education for a New Century* (Washington, DC: Thomas B. Fordham Foundation and the Progressive Policy Institute, 2000).

Chapter 6: Cosmopolitanism

1. Kelly Oliver, *Witnessing: Beyond Recognition* (Minneapolis: University of Minnesota Press, 2001).

2. Becky Petit and Bruce Western, "Mass Imprisonment and the Life Course: Race and Class Inequality in US Incarceration," *American Sociological Review* 69, no. 2 (April 2004): 151–69.

3. Don Terry, "A Gang Gives a Name to Students' Fear: Decepticons," *New York Times*, March 1, 1989.

4. Interview with the author.

5. Posse Foundation, www.possefoundation.org.

6. Interview with the author.

7. Ann Bainbridge Frymier and Paul A. Mongeau, "Differentiating Comfortable from Uncomfortable Teacher-Student Touches II: Hugs, Hits, and Handshakes," paper presented at the Annual Meeting of the Eastern Communication Association, Saratoga Springs, NY, April 23–26, 1998.

8. Kwame Anthony Appiah, *Cosmopolitanism: Ethics in a World of Strangers* (New York: Norton, 1997).

Chapter 7: Context and Content

1. James S. Coleman, "Social Capital in the Creation of Human Capital," *American Journal of Sociology* 94 (1988): 95–120.

2. Alejandro Portes and Patricia Landolt, "The Downside of Social Capital," *American Prospect* 94, no. 26 (1996): 18–21.

3. Ronald S. Burt, *Structural Holes: The Social Structure of Competition* (Cambridge, MA: Harvard University Press, 1992).

4. Émile Durkheim, *The Elementary Forms of the Religious Life* (London: Allen & Unwin, 1912).

Chapter 8: Completion

1. Yoshi Iwasaki, Judith Bartlett, and John O'Neil, "Coping with Stress Among Aboriginal Women and Men with Diabetes in Winnipeg, Canada," *Social Science Medicine* 60, no. 5 (2005): 977–88.

2. Pierre Bourdieu and Loïc Wacquant, *An Invitation to Reflexive Sociology* (Chicago: University of Chicago Press, 1992).

3. Nestor Capoeira, *Capoeira: Roots of the Dance-Fight Game* (Berkeley, CA: North Atlantic Books, 2012), 20.

4. Ruth Stone, *Music in West Africa* (New York: Oxford University Press, 2005).

5. E. N. Walker, *Beyond Banneker: Black Mathematicians and the Paths to Excellence* (Albany: State University of New York Press, 2014).

Chapter 9: Clean

1. Heather L. Stuckey and Jeremy Nobel, "The Connection Between Art, Healing, and Public Health: A Review of Current Literature," *American Journal of Public Health* 100, no. 2 (2010): 254–63.

2. Anne Dalebrough, Thalia R. Goldstein, and Ellen Winner, "Short-Term Mood Repair Through Art-Making: Positive Emotion Is More Effective Than Venting," *Motivation and Emotion* 32 (2008): 288–95.

3. Jill E. Oakes and Rick Riewe, *Spirit of Siberia: Traditional Native Life, Clothing, and Footwear* (Toronto: Bata Shoe Museum Foundation, 1998).

4. Lonna M. Malmsheimer, "'Imitation White Man': Images of Transformation at the Carlisle Indian School," *Studies in Visual Communication* 11, no. 4 (1985): 54–75.

5. Pascal Blanchard et al., eds., *Human Zoos: Science and Spectacle in the Age of Colonial Empires* (Liverpool, UK: Liverpool University Press, 2008).

6. G. McKim-Smith and M. L. Welles, "Material Girls—and Boys: Dressing Up in Cervantes," *Bulletin of the Cervantes Society of America* 24, no. 1 (2004): 66.

7. Fernand Braudel, *Capitalism and Material Life, 1400–1800*, trans. Miriam Kochan (New York: Harper Colophon, 1975), 235.

Chapter 10: Code Switching

1. Kristen Hawley Turner, "Flipping the Switch: Code-Switching from Text Speak to Standard English," *English Journal* 98, no. 5 (2009): 60–65; Mike Baynham, "Code Switching and Mode Switching: Community Interpreters and Mediators of Literacy," in *Cross Cultural Approaches to Literacy*, ed. Brian Street (Cambridge, UK: Cambridge University Press, 1993); Doris A. Flowers, "Codeswitching and Ebonics in Urban Adult Basic Education Classrooms," *Education and Urban Society* 32 (February 2000): 221–36.

2. B. A. Brown, "'It Ain't No Slang That Can Be Said About This Stuff': Language, Identity, and Appropriating Science Discourse," *Journal of Research in Science Teaching* 43, no. 1 (2006): 96–126.

Chapter 11: Curation and Computing

1. Philip Cash Cash, quoted in Christina Kreps, *Liberating Culture: Cross-Cultural Perspectives on Museums, Curation, and Heritage Preservation* (New York: Routledge, 2003), 99.

2. Mizuko Ito et al., *Living and Learning with New Media: Summary of Findings from the Digital Youth Project*, John D. and Catherine T. MacArthur Foundation Reports on Digital Media and Learning (Cambridge, MA: MIT Press, 2009), https://mitpress.mit.edu/sites/default/files/titles/free_download /9780262513654_Living_and_Learning.pdf.

3. Wolff-Michael Roth and Ken Tobin, "Cogenerative Dialoguing and Metaloguing: Reflexivity of Processes and Genres," *Forum Qualitative Sozialforschung/Forum: Qualitative Social Research* 5, no. 3 (2004): art. 7, http:// www.qualitative-research.net/fqs-texte/3-04/04-3-7-e.htm.

Index